DON'T

JUST

~~BREATHE~~

DON'T JUST ~~BREATHE~~

TAKE CONTROL OF YOUR LIFE—OR BE A SPECTATOR

JOHN GRAZIANO

Don't Just Breathe: Take Control of Your Life—or Be a Spectator

Copyright © 2018 John Graziano. All rights reserved. No part of this book may be reproduced or retransmitted in any form or by any means without the written permission of the publisher.

Published by Breathe, LLC
Tucson, Arizona

ISBN: 978-0-692-11935-8 (paperback)
ISBN: 978-0-692-12725-4 (ebook)
LCCN: 2018943471

rev201901

Portions of the proceeds go to the following:

Integrative Touch for Kids (ITK) supports families whose children have any type of special health or medical needs. This includes kids with cancers, genetic conditions, autism, cerebral palsy, traumatic stress, and other health issues.

ITK provides various different integrative healing therapies, such as massage, sound healing, reflexology, energy, equine, play and music therapies through their many programs.

ITK works in both hospital and community settings to change the way people view healthcare.

Thanks to the incredible support of their volunteers and contributors, families receive ITK's healing services free of charge.

www.IntegrativeTouch.org

National Alliance on Mental Illness (NAMI) of Southern Arizona supports a world-class treatment and recovery system for people with mental illness. This includes support groups for family members and friends affected by a loved one with mental illness. NAMI supports the advocacy, education, and raises awareness of the importance of mental health.

www.namisa.org

The information in this book is purely from my own life experiences and from my own analysis of others. The stories of my massage clients are true, names have been left out to maintain their anonymity and privacy.

The suggestions provided in this book are merely playful and humorous tools I have applied for my own purposes.

This book is not intended as a substitute for medical or psychological advice.

CONTENTS

Acknowledgments		ix
Introduction		xi
1	Macho Man	3
2	I Was a Yes Man	25
3	Normal vs. Natural	41
4	Goal vs. Intention	51
5	Your Beliefs Will Carry You	71
6	The Great Director	87
7	Advertising and Media	97
8	Be Comfortable with Being Uncomfortable	111
9	Believe It until You Become It!	131
10	Heroes—Who Needs Them?	141
11	Lucky I Ran into You	155

ACKNOWLEDGMENTS

This book, along with the way I live my life today, would not be possible without my wife, Linda.

She demonstrates unconditional love and shows me how to love myself. She taught me that my unhappy emotions were merely warning signs that I was not being true to myself.

Because of her, I learned how to end my black and white way of thinking. Basically, she inspired me to grow.

My children, every member of my family, friends, massage clients, and even foes were all teachers in my life.

I would also like to thank Wheatmark Publishing for their services. The staff is very knowledgeable and supportive. They took the stressful parts of publishing off my hands so I could focus on the writing. It was effortless. Their services are truly priceless.

I am grateful for having all these people in my life—past, present, and future.

INTRODUCTION

This book was inspired by my life experiences. I have been a massage therapist since 1994, and I have worked for many top resorts. Prior to my massage career, I worked in New York City as a bellman, doorman, waiter, bartender, and security officer. You name it, I did it.

It wasn't until I became a massage therapist that I realized that I can enjoy what I do for a living. I never liked working my other jobs. I figured that is why it is called *work*.

What you will read in this book you already knew as a child. You may have unremembered because of the unwarranted social shackles subconsciously placed on you.

Reading this book will not change your life, nor will any other book you'll ever read. Only you can change your life. If you understand and accept this simple fact, then and only then will you begin the process of transformation. Once you realize this, you will be able to change thoughts,

Introduction

intentions, emotions, goals—basically anything you want to change—at will.

From my experience, there are only two reasons why people turn their lives around. One is because of devastating circumstances, such as a death of someone close, an illness, a loss of job or house, or anything that forces change and a new way of living. The other reason people change is because they really, really fucking want to! I prefer the latter reason.

What if we were to change our lives while we are living it—where we don't have to hit a wall before we change course? It's kind of like sailing on open waters, and as the winds change, so will your course. So, in life, don't wait until you actually *hit* something before you adjust your course. You need to continually navigate.

I was a guy who would blame others for my failures, misfortunes, and other crap in between. I did not want to take charge of my life. The reasons for this are endless, but mainly I was a crowd pleaser. I always felt obligated to please others before myself. I wanted everyone to like me and accept me.

The main reason I didn't take charge of my own life was because if I tried something and failed, I did not want egg on my face. I figured it was better to be a spectator rather than a player. The public can critique a player but never a spectator. How could they critique me? I'm just a spectator. I never did anything wrong, and I never did anything right either.

I took the easy road, at least that is what I thought. It was like giving other people the keys to your car, having them

Introduction

drive you around, and never liking where they brought you. That made me a spectator in my life—my *own* life, and that is sad.

It wasn't until I became a massage therapist that my eyes were opened to people—their behavior and their feelings. I will share some of their stories, along with my own.

I realize that as different as we all are in regard to the paths we take, the lifestyles we lead, and our backgrounds, occupations, and beliefs, we all basically want the same thing. We want to be accepted and loved for who we are, to be ourselves—very simple.

André Gide once said, "It is better to be hated for what you are than to be loved for what you are not."

Think about that for a minute. Imagine that no one has to pretend or wear a mask when they leave their home. This may sound simple enough to do, but why don't we? Could it be vulnerability? I don't know. Our happiness depends on us being ourselves.

I used to look up to people who had their shit together, from common people to celebrities, famous doctors, and speakers. I can tell you from personal experience that these people don't have their shit together. Far from it. I am telling you this not to degrade these people. I'm telling you so you don't put them on a pedestal.

Their lives are an illusion, and so is what the public thinks of them. It's all an act, a *business*, if you will. The best performance you will ever see them in is not in a movie but in an interview. They wish they were the people they portray in the interview.

Of course, there are exceptions. Some have great hearts

Introduction

and integrity, but only a few. Working for hotels in New York City and resorts throughout the country, word gets around who the jerks are and who the good eggs are.

I wrote *Don't Just Breathe* in order for readers to find comforting commonalities. Life can be very challenging at times. I got through it with humor and games. It was a necessity.

For most of my life, I worried about dying. I realize now that it was a waste of time. We start dying the minute we are born, so death should not be our fear. *Not feeling alive* is what one should be fearful of. Mae West said it best: "You only live once, but if you do it right, once is enough."

By writing this book, I want to help others, as well as help *myself*. I know I will pick up this book and read it again when needed, just to keep me in tune. I hope you read and enjoy.

DON'T

JUST

~~BREATHE~~

ID 1

MACHO MAN

To be yourself in a world that is constantly trying to make you something else is the greatest accomplishment.
—Ralph Waldo Emerson

Growing up, I never went for what I really wanted or never even thought to ask myself why I wanted it. I would get sidetracked, perhaps subconsciously.

Seeing movies on the big screen made a big impression on my life. I was amazed by the emotions expressed by the actors and the kids I saw in films. I witnessed emotions I believed I did not possess or was even capable of showing.

I was born in a small town in Sicily called Ciminna. At the age of four, our family left Sicily by ship to move to Brooklyn, New York.

It was a difficult transition for me. The ship voyage from Sicily to New York was one I will never forget. It seemed like yesterday. It was emotional for everyone. We were leaving half our relatives in Sicily to be with the other half in America.

All our belongings were packed in a very large, shiny, metal chest strong enough to withstand anything thrown at it. We also had hard luggage with rope tied around it—not that they needed rope. They seemed strong enough. How we fit all this into small Fiats is still a mystery to me. I assumed every member of my family strapped a piece of luggage to each Fiat.

We boarded the ship and stood outside on the deck, where we waved good-bye to the family we were leaving behind. We were close enough to see their faces and their expressions. I thought this was supposed to be a happy occasion, but it wasn't for the family we were leaving behind. I couldn't understand why they were crying. Their faces were getting smaller and smaller as the ship's distance was getting farther from the dock. Once their faces were not visible anymore, my parents, older brother and sister, and I soon settled into our cabin.

I also remember a particular experience that frightened me nearly to death. It was late in the morning on a clear, sunny day. I heard loud sirens. Shortly after, I saw passengers walking very briskly out of their cabins and heading to the outdoor deck. My family and I also joined the crowd heading out. The crew of the ship started lining us up. Their voices were loud and firm. I could not make out all that they were saying because they were using big words for a four-year-old to understand. They started handing out life jackets for everyone to put on, and I knew something was very wrong. I stood in a line alongside my sister and brother, who were five and six years older than me. Everyone was in a line standing shoulder-to-shoulder. I wasn't quite sure what was going on, but I knew it wasn't good.

I was surprised to see how calm my sister and brother were under these circumstances. I was even more surprised with the expressions on my parents' faces. Their faces showed no fear, as if they were accepting death like war heroes.

Moments later, everyone started to remove their life jackets, and they headed back to their cabins as though this was a dress rehearsal. And indeed, that is exactly what it was—a freakin' drill.

Macho Man

My parents failed to let their four-year-old know that this fiasco he just lived through was a drill and that the ship was not going to sink.

This could have been the start of what would contribute to the lack of emotions I had as I continued growing up.

Things changed quickly for me in this new country. Life was very different from what I was used to—everything from language to culture. I had to adapt quickly, especially to the language.

The only thing that didn't change for me was the food. It tasted the same in America as it did in Sicily, thanks to my mom.

I remember one day in kindergarten enjoying one of my usual lunch meals from home, which was prosciutto and provolone on fresh, crispy Italian bread. Next to me in the cafeteria was a boy eating bologna. In the five years that I had been on this earth, I had never seen bologna before, and from what it looked like, I knew it was a form of meat I did not want to partake of. This boy was very protective of his bologna. As he took it out of his lunchbox, I noticed he guarded his meat with some kind of four-inch-by-four-inch soft white structure to buffer it, which turned out to be white bread. Sliced white bread was foreign to me. As he was eating, I didn't know what to make of it. I remember just staring at this kid's bread for a very long time, like you would stare at a petri dish waiting for bacteria to grow. I even asked him if I could touch his bread with my finger. I was that curious about his bread. He did allow me to touch his bread, and it was fun. What a good kid he was.

School was never easy for me. I attended PS 101 in Brooklyn, or I should say I *showed up* at PS 101 in Brooklyn.

Kindergarten was a breeze for me. After countless months of drawing with crayons and playing with blocks and plastic animals, I was catapulted to first grade. Back in 1968, children didn't learn to read or write until first grade.

First grade was the worst two years of my childhood life. In kindergarten, I never spoke to anyone because I couldn't speak English. The only interaction or any form of communication I received from my classmates was their throwing blocks and plastic animals at me.

I remember my teacher. She introduced me to another boy who spoke Italian and English. I was full of joy and hope. My world just got a lot better. I then had a buddy. I sat with him in front of the classroom at a long table for two students. When the teacher talked, I quickly turned to my left and asked him in Italian, "What did she say?" And he told me. I quickly turned back to the teacher and then right back at him. Again I said, "What did she say?" This went on for weeks. This buddy of mine was my *oracle*. School was still tough, but with this kid I had a fighting chance.

One day it all ended abruptly. The words, "What did she say?" never left my mouth again. My translator (buddy) quit with no notice. After I said my last, "What did she say?" he jumped up from his seat and screamed in Italian, "I can't take this anymore! I can't do my own schoolwork because of you." He stormed to the back of the classroom and sat down at an empty seat.

My teacher didn't speak a word of Italian, but she didn't need to. Universal language kicked in for many of us. I looked at my teacher, and my face said, "What do I do now?" And her face said, "Sorry, kid. You're screwed." I never blamed that kid at all, even right after it happened. I knew at a young age, it was just too much for anyone. That is when I started to suppress my emotions and subconsciously became macho.

Let's examine what *macho* really is. *Macho* is defined as "traditional ideas about what men are like, such as showing noticeable strength and aggression in an exaggerated way." Being macho is not easy. You always have to walk macho, think macho, and act and react macho. But most important it requires considerable mental effort to respond macho in a conversation; therefore, there can be a slight delay when responding. But with practice, delay time can be cut in half.

In this society, guys always have to act like guys and girls like girls. Why can't we mix this up? I think that would be fun.

I mean sometimes a guy can let his guard down a little and simply let go, listen, and feel. We are way too Americanized.

When I visited Italy a few times, I noticed that it would be common for two men to hold hands or wrap arms as they strolled down the street. This didn't necessarily mean that they were gay. They were just showing their friendship.

If you ever watch a Spanish soap opera, you will notice the emotions being expressed by the male actors. You don't necessarily need to understand the words. You can basically form some kind of conclusion by their facial expressions and body language.

If you were to watch an American soap opera, the male actors appear as animated meat (without much expression). This is not a reflection on anyone's acting ability but rather a reflection on our culture.

Boys in our society are taught to be strong, not to feel, not to show emotions, and to never show weakness. All these hidden feelings that boys are forced to keep inside themselves unfortunately show up later in life in the form of depression, which may lead to anger, which may lead to violence.

Big Teddy Bear

A rather big guy came to see me in a hotel for a deep-tissue massage. He was about six foot three, muscular, well built, and very handsome ... kind of reminds me of myself.

Once the massage began, and I started to go deep and heard a noise that I at first thought was a laugh. I asked if he was okay. "I'm fine. You can go even deeper," he said. So I did. What I thought was a laugh turned out to be an angry cry. Again, I stopped and asked if he was okay. "I'm fine. Go deeper!" he said.

With only a couple of years' experience as a massage therapist, I wasn't quite sure what to do. I have had a few females cry on my table before, but never a guy that was six three and 240 pounds, who was capable of bending me into a pretzel if he felt he needed to. At that point I considered myself a reasonable, incredible coward, and I continued so I wouldn't upset him.

He started speaking in fragments. He then raised his voice and started cursing.

I politely asked him if he wanted to end the service. "No. You're doing a great job," he then said. I put myself on

Macho Man

automatic pilot and continued with the massage. When the massage was done, I did not dare to ask him what the fuck that was about. I let him know I was leaving that particular hotel and that he could come to the new spa I would be working at. He did, but only once. Management advised me—*actually made it clear to me*—not to have him come back. I guess the spa walls were too thin.

I then asked if he would like to have massages at my house instead. I knew he would yell and curse in my home, just as he would anywhere else. So I felt I needed to inform my wife of his behavior during the massage so she wouldn't call a hostage negotiator in the middle of my service. I only told her that the guy who was coming over likes to yell and curse during his massage. I said that as if it was no big thing, as if this was common to do. Yeah, four out of ten people do this kind of stuff. I also ordered her not to come down to the basement whatsoever—*under no circumstances*—just like Dr. Frankenstein did when he was secretly building his monster in his lab.

My massages were the only thing that would help this man. He slowly gave me more information about himself as he got to know me better. In a nutshell, this man didn't like (friggin' hated) his parents.

He once showed up to my house with a crew cut. He normally had long hair to his shoulders. I noticed he had a long scar on top of his head, and I innocently asked him how he got that. "A bullet," he replied. I knew he wasn't joking either. He said, "It was a drug deal that went bad." He walked me out to his car to show me bullet holes all over the driver's side. There were a lot of them.

I can't imagine the life this guy had. He may have fallen

into the category I mentioned earlier—how not feeling may turn into depression, anger, and then violence.

This man became a good friend of mine. I never looked at him negatively for the actions he took in his life. I only saw who he was as I knew him. He later moved two thousand miles away for a good job opportunity.

I find from my experience that the bigger and badder guys look on the outside, deep down they also have the biggest hearts too.

Cold Crab Cakes

A man who was about seventy years old came to me for a massage. He was soft-spoken and seemed very calm. When I asked what kind of massage he wanted, his reply was "I don't care." I asked if there was anything that he wanted me to focus on. He said no. I then asked if he was there to relax or if he wanted *deep tissue*. He said again, "I don't care." His answers, or lack of answers, were only making my massage more difficult. I had no idea what this guy wanted.

He never said a word as I was massaging. I never even asked how my pressure was because I knew he would not have an answer for that either. After thirty minutes, he stated, "I hope you don't think I'm an asshole."

"Of course not. Why would I think that?" I said.

He said, "I learned something in my later life that I wish I would have learned earlier." He proceeded to inform me that he had learned how to let go of control.

He had a successful business, made a lot of money, had a few homes, and traveled regularly. But he was never happy

Macho Man

until he learned to let go. He never mentioned how or why this transformation occurred.

He said everything in his life was *his way or the highway*. It wasn't until later that he realized that he made everyone around him uncomfortable, including his employees, friends, and even relatives. He admitted that he was mean, short-tempered, and very unpleasant to be around.

He shared a story about meeting a friend he had not seen in a while for lunch. They both ordered the same item for lunch—crab cakes. Once the crab cakes were served, they started to eat them. His friend asked him if they were cold in the middle. He replied, "No. They are hot." His friend said, "Why would my crab cakes be cold and yours not? We both ordered the same thing." My client told his friend to let the waiter know so he could correct the problem.

Well, the topic of this lunch meeting they planned turned out to be all about the lunch they were eating instead of catching up on each other's lives.

I always preach to people to live in the present, even when eating their meals. I tell them to enjoy every bite. So who am I to complain about this guy complaining about his cold crab cakes? Touché for him. He was living in the present every time he took a bite of those damn cold crab cakes.

My client's friend was taking this very personally, and it was on the way to ruining the rest of his day. My client tried to have him think logically about the situation. "It's not like the staff spotted you as you walked into the restaurant and tried to deliberately screw you. It's only a mistake that happened, and it could easily be fixed." But his friend was not ready to accept it at that time. Oh well.

Again, this man I massaged never shared how he transformed or what the reason was for his transformation. But he was happier in this stage of his life than he ever had been before. He said he enjoyed traveling and was appreciative of everything he had and whatever this universe bestowed on him. It is very encouraging to know that this nice, gentle, caring, compassionate, grateful, and loving man was once a blowhard.

Typhoid Billy

There is nothing anyone can learn from this particular story, except that we have some people who do very strange things in this world.

A young man in his early twenties came into the spa. He had an appointment for a massage, but he was also interested in becoming a massage therapist himself, so he had many questions. I always welcome and enjoy giving information to people who are interested in what I do. He appeared shy and had sensitive eyes. I liked the way he looked at me.

When I started to massage him, he began to make cow sounds. These sounds started very low. I assumed that his breathing simply sounded similar to cow sounds, and I just went with it. However, cow sounds rapidly escalated to actual really loud cow sounds. At this point, I had to ask if everything was okay. He replied yes. However, he did not stop making these sounds, and they only got louder after I asked him if everything was okay.

In all honesty, I really didn't care what sounds people made while in a massage, even mooing. But I had to wonder what someone would think if loud cow sounds came out of a room where a massage service was in progress. So, for the sake of the spa and its clients there, I had to put an end to it. He was so loud that I knew my manager would have knocked on my door.

I asked him, "Can you please stop making loud cow sounds?" I didn't ask him *why*. That was none of my business. I just needed him to stop! "I feel vulnerable, and this is my way of feeling safe," he said. Sweet fancy Moses, I thought to myself. I assured him that he was in a safe place, and I thought to myself that a psychiatric hospital would be even safer. So he stopped and did not utter a sound or a word for the rest of the treatment.

Once the massage was over, he asked if I could walk him to the bathroom. I informed him it was the last door on the right just before the lobby. For some reason, he insisted that I walk with him there.

When he got to the bathroom door, he walked in, turned toward me, stared at me with a smile similar to Jack Nicholson in the movie *The Shining*, and slowly closed the door. When he was finished in the bathroom, he left the spa. As he exited the spa door, he stared once more at me as he closed the door. He did not tip, and I was not surprised.

I went to use the restroom after he left, and I noticed he didn't flush after he took a big dump. I guess that would explain the loud cow sounds. But seriously folks, I think that's because I did not allow him to make loud cow sounds during his massage. Leaving that monumental dump was his way of saying, "I own you, bitch."

A few days later, I'm pretty sure I gave his mom a

massage. This woman entered my room, with a high amount of energy and speaking very loudly. She told me she was stressed out because her sister just died. "Oh my God, I'm so sorry. Was she sick?" I said, looking at her with compassion.

"No. She died from a backhoe (excavating machine that digs into the ground) accident." I continued to look at her a bit puzzled, but still with a look of compassion. "Don't worry. I didn't like her anyway. I'd like you to spend most of the time on my shoulders," she said. Those words left her mouth with no hesitation or feelings whatsoever! It was as though she was ordering the soup du jour. I never said a word during the massage and neither did she. Thank God.

I can't imagine what a typical day is like for people like this. If my encounter for an hour with them is like this, what does their day look like from the time they have their first cup of coffee to the time they put their head on that pillow? It's scary knowing that they drove to the appointment on their own.

Too Macho

Many men do not want a male therapist to work on them. Maybe they are insecure with their sexuality, or maybe they just prefer to have a female for whatever reason.

But some of these men just don't want another man working on them. I will make this clear for the guys who insist on female therapists. The female therapists really don't want to work on you unless you are Brad Pitt or George Clooney. Female therapists would rather work on other females.

Macho Man

If a man shows any indication of being a creep, jerk, or sleaze, they will talk about him in the breakroom and inform the other female therapists who may have the pleasure of massaging him.

There are times when couples want a couple's massage in the same room. Most couples do not have a preference of the gender of the therapist. Their only concern is that they get a good massage.

Sometimes a couple will request having two female therapists to work on them. They usually make it very clear to be sure that there will be no mistakes in the booking.

Let me give you a quick bio on the couple who typically request this. These men come in with a female companion who is a third of their age and are old enough to be her father or even grandfather. These men seem to be insecure with having another male massaging his companion.

In situations where the male client was told that two female therapists were not available, he would then request that the male therapist be unattractive. I'm shitting you negative. This stuff happens.

Who am I to judge? If I won the lottery, you may even see me going to a resort with a spring chicken.

Many times when I would greet my male client in the waiting room, he would be reluctant to have me as his therapist. He would say aloud that he requested a *female* therapist, just so everyone in the spa lobby would know his level of macho-ism. Some of these men will reluctantly agree to having me massage them.

Well, let me tell you, half of these guys open up to me. They get comfortable and share their stories and express their feelings. That makes me feel good. It shows how comfortable someone who was resistant can become in my presence.

Unfortunately, almost all the men who opened up to me would try to avoid me the next day. It was as if we had an experimental sexual encounter of some kind, and he was ashamed. Oh well.

Matthew McConaughey Called Out!

One time I went to greet a woman who specifically asked for a male therapist. This is common because they want someone with strong hands. In this case, she wanted a better-looking male therapist too.

When I called her name in the spa lobby, she did not get up. I went back two minutes later and called her name again. Still no one stood up. Someone, who I assumed was her friend, pointed to her and said that that was her.

I said, "Are you Catherine?" She didn't say yes. I'd had my body scanned by machines in hospitals and airports before, but never in as much detail as with this woman's eyeballs. She started scanning me from my face to my feet and back up to my face, twice the speed of a snail, all this time in the presence of a spa lobby full of guests who were observing me like a one-man Broadway show.

She looked at me and said out loud, "I was expecting Matthew McConaughey." And I was expecting Jennifer Aniston, so just get on my damn table, and let's get this over with. Oh man, I wish I could have said that to her without getting fired!

Instead, being quick-witted, I said, "Matthew called in

sick today, and I'm covering his shift." I figured that statement would not get me fired and would break the ice.

She stood up reluctantly and followed me to the massage room as though I was taking her to the gas chamber in Auschwitz. Keep in mind, this woman was no prize herself. She had a face you would find in a chum bucket.

The massage didn't go that well either. There was no flow in this massage. She kept passing gas, and it would take about a minute or two for me to regain my motor skills each time she did. I wish I'd had one in my chamber so I could show her who's boss, but I was empty.

This is the kind of shit we therapists have to put up with. I could make a movie or a sitcom on these nuts that infiltrate these kinds of "rehab resorts."

I Would Have Canceled

I once found myself in an embarrassing situation where I could not have felt any less macho.

I went to a chiropractor who I visit often. His office is set up with a waiting area by the front desk and two room dividers separating the waiting area and six treatment tables, which were all occupied at the time.

When it was time to work on me, he did the usual moves I was familiar with. The last move he does is the worst because it resembles a move that Hulk Hogan would use to pin you down for the count.

As he finishes this particular move, I heard a very loud and long sound that could wake a man out of a coma. It took me a second or two to realize it was flatulence suddenly and relentlessly released. I was in shock that this person didn't have the decency to hold it in until he exited the office.

After I sat up from that Hulk Hogan move, I noticed that everyone was staring at me as if they were waiting for me to finish a eulogy. It also took a second or two to realize it was me. I heard giggles and a few laughs. I got up and walked to the front office, where other patients in the waiting area also giggled.

I paid my bill like a man and walked toward the front door, which seemed at the time like the length of a football field. I drove home with only two thoughts. The first one was that I needed to find a new chiropractor, and the other was how I could not have known I had gas. I would have canceled my appointment just like any decent human being would have if I'd known.

Okay! I'm a Man of God

I sat down to eat my lunch in the breakroom of a large and busy chiropractic office where I worked. I was very tired from all the massages I'd just given.

In the breakroom were three chiropractors and three massage therapists, including me. One of the chiropractors was fairly new, and everyone was afraid of him, not because he was mean but only because he looked mean. He was bald with a big frame and resembled a famous professional wrestler known as George "The Animal" Steele.

I was so tired that I put my lunch down in front of me and rested my head down, eyes closed, arms leaning around my lunch. Before I took my first bite, I heard George say,

Macho Man

"Now there's a good man!" I thought I walked in and interrupted a conversation. I noticed he was staring at me. I looked back at him puzzled. He continued to preach to me and everyone else in that breakroom that I was the only one who was grateful for what the good Lord placed in front of me. George also noted that there weren't many men like me around me anymore.

After his sermon, I didn't dare to tell him the truth. I only put my head down because I was really tired. So I played along and along and along. In the days ahead, it got to the point where my coworkers would enter the break room just to see me start my lunch, even though they didn't have anything to eat. They just enjoyed watching me trying to act religious. Within a couple of weeks, there was much rejoicing among the staff because George got transferred to a different location. He was a difficult person to work with.

I know I preach about being honest to everyone, but please cut me some slack in this case.

LIRR

I was taking the Long Island Rail Road home from Manhattan to Lindenhurst. I was on the 3:00 p.m. train, which meant there were a lot of construction workers who rode at that time, and they enjoyed drinking their beers.

Back then, passengers were allowed to bring alcohol on the train. I'm not sure if that is the case now. I was sitting on the aisle seat, and there were two seats on my left that were occupied by two bozos who'd had too much to drink.

The train stopped at Lindenhurst, which is where I had to get off. I was in a deep sleep, which was common on the

LIRR. I was rudely awakened by the bozos because this was their stop also and could not get past me because I am six three. They finally got me up from a deep sleep by lifting me out of my seat, literally by my arm and jacket, and called me an asshole.

I started to run to catch the door before it closed. Within the first step that I took, I noticed that my leg had fallen asleep, and I started to drag my leg while running for the door. The train doors closed, and I missed my stop, along with those bozos. They were behind me in the aisle, also trying to reach the door. When I turned to get back in my seat, they approached me full of apologies and compassion. That is when I realized that these two bozos noticed my leg dragging and mistakenly assumed I was a person with a physical disability.

Now I had no choice. If I told them the truth, they would have thrown me out the window between stops. The three of us took our seats again and got off at Babylon station so we could catch the next train back to Lindenhurst.

By this time, my leg wasn't asleep anymore, but I had to fake it. I limped back into the train, then out of the train, then to the platform, down the stairs, and to my car. This was the only logical option.

Thank God I didn't see anyone I knew; otherwise, they would have asked, "What the fuck happened to your leg?"

Flip-Flops for Every Macho Man

"Hey, man. I don't want any trouble. Okay?"
"Let's just relax and enjoy our lives."
"Let's respect each other. No conflict."

Macho Man

"No need to fear for any of us."
"Peace, brother."

Those are the thoughts and the attitude of the state of mind I am in when I leave my house when wearing flip-flops. There is no way not to have this attitude while wearing flip-flops. Not much can happen. Only peace and love.

When I leave my house wearing sneakers, who knows what's in store for me? I am ready to chase or be chased. I am ready to defend myself instead of trying to make peace with the antagonist. Basically, I am prepared to do whatever I can to protect myself, stand up for my personal beliefs, and attend protests, even though I don't know what I am protesting. Just let me know when, where, and what time. *Why* isn't important if I were wearing comfortable sneakers.

When I wear steel-tipped boots, I just want to kick guys in the balls. What else can you do with steel-tipped shoes besides engross yourself in some type of hard labor where the chances of a heavy object falling on your foot is fairly high? You can't run or relax in them.

I do not consider myself a violent person. I'm sure the pope is not a violent person either. However, if he were to put on steel-toed boots, he may entertain the thought of kicking a cardinal in the nuts. Maybe that's why monks wear sandals and UPS robes. So they don't get violent toward each other.

So, if world leaders, government officials, and military personnel were to wear flip-flops and seamless robes, we may no longer have a need for such high-powered positions or even a need for power.

2

I WAS A YES MAN

*It is better to be hated for
what you are than to be loved
for what you are not.*
—André Gide

I wish I would have been more of myself to others. I was a stiff for most of my life, never wanting to give my opinion, even when asked. I can tell you with great conviction that I am now the complete opposite. I don't worry very much about what people think, but at the same time, I try to be conscious not to hurt anyone's feelings.

In the past, I always wanted to be nice to everyone. But I didn't know the true meaning of what *nice* was. I was under the impression that *nice* was an emotion you give to someone and then expect that same emotion to come back to you from that same person. If I were on a hiking trail and said good morning to another hiker passing by, I would expect a cheery good morning back. And if I didn't get that bit of kindness back, I just couldn't understand why not. I felt that I was at least owed that much.

Let's analyze this using money as an example. If I were to give you a check for one hundred dollars, I sincerely would want you to cash that check, have fun, and enjoy. However, at the same time, I would anxiously await the day you give a check for one hundred dollars back to me so I could use it to make myself happy. This does not make any sense for either party involved because truthfully you already have within you what will make you happy. What

I am saying is that I eventually learned to put my happiness in my own hands.

There is a saying, "Give a man a fish, and he will eat for a day; teach a man to fish, and he will eat for a lifetime." So what if I learned how to be happy on my own without the help of others? No, I am not saying that I needed to be a hermit, far from that. I am saying that I started being comfortable with myself and realizing that happiness starts from inside me.

Later in this book in "The Great Director" chapter, I mentioned that at the age of twelve I met a new, great friend who was funny and full of life. I also mentioned that I wanted to spend as much time as I could with him. Why? Because I felt happy around him. He took me away from my serious life that I had become accustomed to at home. I did not plan to marry him! I did not attempt to arrange my parents to adopt him so he could spark up my family's life. What I wanted to do was to *learn* from him—to get inside his head!

I was willing and truly needed to change myself and my attitude. So I carried what I learned from him and others and modified my view of life and how I interacted in it.

I sometimes think I went overboard with this comical view of the world I now have. If you were to ask me thirty years ago if I had a chance to interview an important figure who passed away, I would have said someone like Lincoln, Gandhi, or Einstein. If you were to ask me the same question today, I would say Curly from *The Three Stooges*.

To sum this up, I had to learn how to make myself happy. It's great to hang around with funny, easy-going, optimistic people, but really it is even better to learn from them, just like it's better to fish for yourself rather than people giving you fish to eat every day.

I went to the waiting area to call out my client's name, and she jumped up from the comfortable chair she was sitting in and briskly walked toward me, shook my hand, and asked me how my day was going. I jokingly said, "That's exactly what we ask our clients."

A few minutes into our massage, before I even got a chance to ask her how the pressure was, she asked me if I was doing okay. I never want to give unsolicited advice to anyone, but in this rare case I felt I had to. I had to because I saw in her what I see in some other people, but most of all I saw in her how I was in my own life. A pleaser. A yes man.

So I politely told her that she needed not worry about me, that I was just doing my job, and she could focus on herself and her needs.

She expressed that her whole life she always put other people's needs before her own. She also said that she answers yes to a request for a favor even before the person finishes asking her. She then gets mad at herself for this pattern that she can't seem to break. She further stated that since people know that she will always say yes, her friends, relatives, and coworkers always go to her when they want help.

As she was telling me all this, I could not wait to tell her *my* story because she pretty much just described me as I was about five years earlier. Man, and did I lay it on her.

I told her this: My first and most important step was to blame myself for being that way. I realized that unless I took full responsibility, I would never be able to change a thing. I was the one who allowed this to happen. And only I could change me.

So I incorporated my two-second rule into my life, which means to wait two seconds before I answer someone who is asking me for a favor. Two seconds may seem long, and it is when someone is waiting for your answer. But with practice, those two seconds can be shortened to one second.

This two-second rule I speak of is a pattern breaker. It breaks down a pattern that I developed throughout my life, which was to answer right away. Growing up, I learned that I had to make other people happy, and one way of doing that was to just say yes to anyone's request without considering my own desires.

Before we go further, I want to make something very clear to the reader. This is the beauty of the birth of anyone's new life—not just with this two-second rule, but with anything in life that needs to be changed. Changing your unhelpful habits is crucial to your growth.

This quote from Ralph Waldo Emerson that states it very clearly: "Sow a thought and you reap an action, sow an action and you reap a habit, sow a habit and you reap a character, sow a character and you reap a destiny."

Another earth-shattering realization I am somewhat embarrassed to have learned this late in my life was that I did not have to give a yes or a no answer when someone asked me for a favor.

One time someone asked me if I could help her move her furniture on an upcoming Saturday. I told her I was scheduled to work that day and would not be able to take the time off. I never said an actual *yes* or an actual *no*. This simple discovery was paramount to me because I was

I Was a Yes Man

always taught to do for others before I do for myself. No was never an option for me up to this point. I felt like this was a revelation! To me, saying no was like saying *fuck off*. Now, I never have to say no to anyone when they ask me for a favor. I just let them know the reason why I can't, and I don't have to say fuck off.

I also expressed to this client that I now have less friends in my life and more acquaintances, and that is a good thing for me. I began what I called a filtration process for my friendships. I looked back to my relationships and figured out who liked me for my companionship and who like me for what I could do for them. I didn't need to be Sherlock Holmes to figure this one out.

Very leisurely, I started to detach myself from those friends that liked me for what I did for them. This process was so slow and gradual that I think it took them a year for them to feel the difference in our relationship. I don't recommend anyone who wants to try this to give the middle finger to these kinds of friends. It's best to be civilized.

This now leaves me with more quality time with true good friends and more time with myself to do the things I love to do most, which is to go hiking deep in the mountains where it's so quiet you can hear your own heartbeat. I sometimes stumble across rare Native American pottery. Once I found a complete jar from the Hopi tribe that contained two tickets to the Ice Capades.

I'm not being mean, but as I get older, I've become more selective. I want to continue making good "films" and don't have as much time left. So I want to surround myself with a good crew for my finale.

This client of mine was very apprehensive about

applying this two-second rule. I massaged her two days later, and she was delighted with her results. She practiced it with her husband for a full day, and the following day she practiced it with other guests in the resort. She acted as if I gave her a magic wand of some sort. There's no magic or trickery here at all. I had to learn this two-second rule many years ago when I lived in the South, but not for the same purpose that I spoke about.

Unbeknown to me, I was acting rude to the older women who would come in for massages when I lived in Georgia. One woman, who I assumed must have taught southern hospitality at a community college, steered me straight. She observed that I was interrupting her as she was still speaking to me. At this time I thought that it was an inaccurate observation on her part and that this old bat was just looking for a confrontation, which at the time I was up for. Politely and innocently, I asked, "How am I being rude?"

"You should wait until I stop talking to respond," she said.

I replied, "Yes, that's because I knew what you were about to say before you stopped talking."

She answered, "Here in the South, it is customary to have a pause for a second before the other person responds."

Innocently again, I said, "Oh, I'm sorry. I didn't know that. I'm not familiar with that because in New York, where I'm from, if there is any pause at all in the conversation, that means one of us is boring and we need to put a kibosh on this chitchat. So I didn't want to be rude to you or anyone else I speak to." She understood what I said, and she took no offense to my action. After thinking about what she said, I realized that the old bat was right. I was being rude.

Tennessee Flat-Top Box

Shortly after moving west from the eastern part of the country, I received a phone call from my first in-home massage client. She got my phone number from a chiropractic office where I left some cards. I let my wife know the good news, that I just had a very sweet old woman who lives in a nursing home call me requesting weekly massages. Since this woman had been receiving weekly massages, she let me know not to bring anything but myself. She had the table, sheets, lotion, and music. The fact that she had everything was a big plus for me because I wouldn't have to schlep my crap through the parking lot and building.

She said she would be sitting on a bench outside the building waiting for me so I wouldn't have a hard time finding her place. Her appointment was at 8:00 p.m. It was dark. While driving into the parking lot, I noticed an older woman sitting on a bench. She was wearing black tights with a cherry red sweater and a black, fluffy hat with sequins. I thought, "Cool. This place has some kind of karaoke or open-mic night for its residents." As I entered the building, she called out my name. We said our introductions and made our way to her place. She had enough perfume on to leave a puddle. I also did not notice any indication of any karaoke or open-mic event. I assumed this seventy-ish-year-old woman just enjoyed dressing like Britney Spears.

The massage table was already set up for me. I approached the table to raise the height because it was too low for me. The oils and lotion were placed on the end table. On the massage table itself was a feather duster. I casually threw it on the couch.

"You're going to need that," she said.

"Need what?" I replied.

"That feather duster."

"What for?"

"You're going to massage me with it."

My exact comment to her was, "Are you shittin' me?" The next three minutes of our conversation was about this feather duster and how it had no therapeutic value in my line of work. She insisted that it was the only thing that relaxes her before the massage itself, and that every male therapist she ever hired was willing to use it.

I felt as if she would be insulted if I didn't. So we agreed to its use for five minutes only. While I was raising the height of the table, she put on some music. I had heard diverse music played during massages before, but never Johnny Cash's "Tennessee Flat-Top Box." When I turned around, this old kook was dancing in the corner of the room not wearing a stitch. It was a style of dancing I had never seen before. It seemed like a cross between the *Charleston* and *tap dancing*. I kept staring at her while she was dancing. Not because I was enthralled, but because my brain could not process what my eyes were seeing. She stared back at me with a forced smile, as though she was a contestant on *Dancing with the Stars* and I was a judge.

I told her I was ready for her to get on the massage table. She refused to be covered. I told her she had to in order for me to massage her. She raised her voice slightly to let me know that other male therapists massaged her in the nude, and she didn't understand why I could not.

So I agreed to it. FYI: In this situation if the genders were reversed, the female therapist could just leave the building or hotel and tell the staff or call for help. Everyone would believe the female therapist over the older male pervert client. But in my situation, not so much. I did not want to have her scream bloody murder and then I end up in the local news. So that's why I agreed to it.

As I began massaging with the feather duster, I remember looking out the window to the downtown city lights and thinking, I can't believe I'm fucking doing this. In this situation, I was forced to be a yes man.

From the stories she told me about this nursing home, the GM must have been Caligula. The only thing that turned me on during this entire experience was Johnny Cash's music. Hearing "Tennessee Flat-Top Box" always reminds me of that sweet, old kook.

Swanky Hotels

Swanky hotels are full of yes men. The employees there are trained to be yes men. But honestly, how much smoke can they blow up your ass before you've had enough?

They make you feel extra special. The staff calls you by your name each time you turn a corner. I guess this is what you are paying for. I'm not sure why that would turn anyone on. Give me a nice, clean hotel, and I will take care of my own self-esteem.

Why do we need a total stranger to make us feel special? This is an honest question I am asking.

Everyone, including the doormen, front-desk personnel, bellmen, and servers are paid to be extra, extra nice to you. Their niceness depends on how much money you paid. Just think, a total stranger giving you so much love. So they don't give you love because of the person you are but because of the money you have.

I have a feeling that with time there will be fewer of these swanky hotels. I think the millennials are not going to buy what these hotels are selling. I predict there will be chains of hotels called Civilized Hotel, where they provide all the accommodations of a swanky hotel but without the bullshit.

I once worked at a top resort with a massage therapist who I will call Biff. Biff treated every client like he/she was a rock star. During the massages he gave, he would name all the muscles he was working on and gave erroneous advice. He would diagnose each client and inform them that his massages were superior to the other therapists in the resort. His clients would receive the best massage because Biff told them so, and they bought it.

I, personally, along with other people, can smell this kind of bullshit. How can anyone accept this kind of patronage from a total stranger? It didn't matter if you were a missionary worker or a child molester, you would be patronized the same.

If you were to be a fly on a wall in Biff's room and you observed the same compliments that Biff dished out to other clients over and over again, would it not negate your entire experience with Biff?

This same story can be applied to many professions. People choose doctors, dentists, lawyers, financial advisors, contractors, and basically any professionals simply because they are nice. This topic comes up with some of the clients I've worked on, and they concur with this concept. I had a financial advisor who told me there was a guy in his office who was quite incompetent and couldn't manage a game of Monopoly. However, because he had a great personality and had the ability to make people feel good, they would trust him with their money.

People choose behavioral health counselors because they are nice to them and they enjoy their company. That's great for others, but for me, give me a counselor who is a straight-shooter so I can accept the information and begin my healing process. I realize that some of the topics people have while going to counseling are very sensitive and do take time. I understand. But minor issues can be blown out of proportion.

Bob, one of my best friends entering college together, never spoke to me until our senior year. He wasted a good portion of his college life seeking counseling, all because I stole his string his freshman year. I couldn't help myself. I'd never seen string like this before. This string should have had its own category—something between string and rope. We reconciled just before our graduation. I gave him half back.

Let's Just Be Civilized!

By this time, you probably think I'm a cold person because you've been reading about why we shouldn't be nice to each other. That is not what my intention is. My intention is for us to live life not wanting or expecting *fish* from anyone.

I had an experience that ended this fiasco with my

yes-man mentality. This was the pivotal point where I decided to stop trying to help everyone under the sun. I had a neighbor who lived two houses down from me who was in her late thirties. She was also in her late seventies. It all depended on how much help she needed from me.

When I moved into the neighborhood, she came over and introduced herself. She was wearing a nightgown with little colorful flowers printed on it. She moved slowly and steadily. She seemed like a nice lady, and we would often talk when we would see each other.

As we became better acquainted, she started to ask for favors. It began with moving some of her furniture, some landscaping, and fixing items in her house. The more I did, the more she asked of me. And like a buffoon, I did it.

I felt bad for this woman living all alone. I sometimes would see her organizing her garage and struggling with even the smallest boxes. At times she seemed so frail that I thought she would collapse under her own weight.

There was another neighbor of mine who I never met. She looked similar to this older woman I described. She had the same hairstyle and height. But I never got a good look at her face because I only saw her when she was jogging by. She was in great shape. She carried weights in both hands. So, if I saw out of my window the older woman working in her yard, I would go over to help. Like a crack detective, it only took me months to come to the realization that the young woman jogging and the old woman I always helped were the same. I could not believe it. It was like watching a thriller when only at the end of the movie do you realize the deception that you just witnessed. My major in college was criminal justice. Go figure!

I Was a Yes Man

I got bamboozled. But how? I consider myself to be very street smart, and I am able to smell someone's bullshit from a mile away. I got suckered because I did not want to believe it. I already formed a relationship with this helpless old woman. I could not see things clearly. Now that I think back, I remember a small part of my brain thinking, this old woman is the same person as that young chick who runs in spandex with weights in her hands. But the larger part of my brain poo-pooed that thought to protect my ego so it would not look dumb.

I then made a conscious effort not to help her anymore. If I saw her working on her yard, I figured she could ask that young lady who runs with weights to help her since they were such good friends.

Time had passed since we had not spoken—not that we had an argument or anything. It was just that I didn't want to help her anymore.

One day she approached me and asked me if I could build something for her. I reluctantly agreed only because I hadn't done anything for her in a while and also because of the fact that her project was not a big job at all.

When I left her house and entered my front door, I felt an uncomfortable feeling in my gut. I knew it was because I agreed to do something I didn't want to do. So I called her on the phone to let her know that I changed my mind about the project. She did not take this lightly. She raised her voice and told me how much this meant to her. I apologized and simply advised her to have someone else do it for her. She went berserk on the phone, as if I promised her I would be a liver donor for her and then canceled the morning of the surgery.

Now, to spare you the details, I will not go any further with our conversation, only that it started with her asking me for the television back she had given me a year prior, which I did not want and never even used. I told her, "I will, as soon as you pay me for all the work I have done at your house." I think you can guess on your own the result of this intellectual conversation. She moved a couple of months later to a different part of the country.

This event was the turning point of my decision not to be overly nice and a yes man to everyone I meet. This is when I started to evaluate my *friendship filter*. But out of all of this, I found something interesting and surprising. The less obligated I felt to help people, the more I wanted to help them.

3

NORMAL VS. NATURAL

*He is richest who is content
with the least, for content is
the wealth of nature.*
—*Socrates*

To me, this is an important topic since this is the main reason many people are living these external, crazy lives from which no good will ever come.

If you were to look up *normal* in a dictionary, it would read something like this: "agreeing with the standards; conforming with the standards." The word *natural* in the same dictionary would be defined as: "not altered; freedom from anything artificial; produced from nature; and something that comes naturally."

Now, I don't know how, when, or why our society got these two words mixed up, but we did. We have done this to ourselves, and we need to reverse this behavior if we want to live a natural life.

Most of us strive to live a normal, artificial—in this case—life, when instead it would be best to strive to live a natural life. I find many people are trying to live their lives the way other people live their lives because that is what normal people do. Now that sentence didn't make much sense as I wrote it on paper. It made less sense when I repeated it aloud. It makes even less sense when I tried to actually live this way.

We act as we do for a combination of reasons, including the media, advertising, and our beliefs and society, all of which I write about. You will find that in every situation in our lives, the issue of normal and natural will be present for the most part.

Keeping Up with the Joneses

Who do we think we are? Rockefellers? How did we get to the point that we have to have everything the rich have and do things the rich do? I remember growing up in Brooklyn. If someone bought a new car, they were *rich*. Everyone else bought used cars. If a family went on vacation by plane and stayed in hotels, they were rich. If you weren't rich, your family would travel by car and stay with family or friends. Back then, we knew what we could and couldn't afford.

If someone in our neighborhood back then spent more money than he earned, he would be considered *the village idiot*. Today, not so much—because it's normal. Back then, people would save money to go on vacation. Now people vacation and find a way to pay it back by working extra. Most kids back then had more sense than some adults do now. Our heads weren't as programmed from outside influences as much as they are now.

When I was a kid, I would go down the block to buy a snack. I would reach into my pocket, discern the amount of funds I possessed, and within seconds, like a financial genius, I was able to calculate the necessary capital needed to purchase that particular item. If I did not have enough funds to buy what I wanted, I would buy an item that I could afford. It was simple to figure out.

The advertising companies have programmed us to think that we could have it all. They make us believe that

Normal vs. Natural

if we do not buy what they are selling, we are simply losers. This goes back to the normal and natural way of thinking. We have conformed with the standards.

As a massage therapist, I hear the same stories from different clients I see on a regular basis. They tell me how much happier they were when they lived in an average house in an average neighborhood, drove an average car, and enjoyed their average lifestyle.

Years later, some of these same clients now have different lifestyles. They now have bigger positions at work, bigger houses in better neighborhoods, better cars—basically better and bigger everything. They also have a bigger fear of losing it.

When they lived in average homes, they would spend quality time with friends. Now with this lifestyle, they use their houses to entertain people, usually with fancy cheeses and expensive chow and top-shelf spirits.

They went from using their homes for friendship to using them for business purposes to impress people and see who can outdo the other.

For example, I picked up my client in the waiting area, a woman in her early fifties. I usually greet clients with a gentle and calming smile, but I got no smile back. That's okay with me. Everyone has bad days. However, once she entered my massage room, she quickly told me she was very stressed and that was why she was there at the resort. I simply said, "I'm so sorry—"

Before I finished, she interrupted and got a little emotional and informed me that her husband lost his job and it had taken a financial toll on them. I knew she was about to spill her guts, so I allowed her to do so before I asked her to lay on my table. I couldn't just say, "Okay. Start face down, and you can tell me when I come back in." That would have been too cold of me.

So I just listened. I had seen her movie before. She was very upset and sad that she lost a lot of her friends once her husband no longer held a job that permitted them to entertain in the way I just described. They had to sell their expensive home and expensive cars and go back to living the average life. They no longer could afford to entertain like before; therefore, they no longer got invited to their so-called friends' homes anymore. She was so caught up in this dilemma that the realization that these so-called friends were never friends to begin with never occurred to her. They were only work associates, and that's all. When I told her this, she looked ashamed as to why she didn't see it this way before. I told her this situation is common and people usually can't see this because they don't look at it this way as it is happening.

National Geographic

I noticed something years back while watching television—something that I had seen many times before but never observed it the way I did as a younger man. Why would I?

I was watching the National Geographic Channel, and they were showing people living in villages made of sticks and mud. They showed their culture: how they socialized, how they hunted, and the kind of homes they lived in.

I must have seen programs similar to this a dozen times before but never thought much about it. Being older and

Normal vs. Natural

being a massage therapist for many years, I developed a sense of people and how to read them.

So here I am, watching these villagers, and it hits me like a ton of bricks in slow motion. I studied their faces, their expressions, their body language, and I noticed that none of these people looked *stressed*. None of these people looked *angry*. None of them showed *fear* in their eyes.

Let's make something clear here. These are the same people who have to hunt for food. They have only feet for transportation. They live in homes made of sticks, grass, and mud and can be destroyed with a heavy storm at any given time.

We have grocery stores, clothing stores, every form of transportation from bikes to planes. We live in homes with appliances and running water. So why are we the ones who live in fear, sadness, anger, and stress? One would think it would be the other way around, but it's not.

Perhaps it's because they are living in the present. Perhaps it's because they are spiritually connected, and our society is spiritually deprived. Maybe people in our society are upset because of the inequality we live with. I think inequality plays a major part in people's unhappiness and anger. I have read various studies showing that countries with very little inequality are happier as a society.

The people in these villages don't take any kind of medication for stress or depression. How screwed up is that? I have a suspicion that we do it to ourselves.

We are always in pursuit of the future, which means that the present rarely exists or it is not important to us anymore. We don't have the time to do the things we enjoy because we work so much. And why do we work so much?

Someone told me a story that sums up what I just stated. I'm not sure if it's a true story or a folktale, but nevertheless it makes a strong statement.

A man leaves his country for America for a better life. He leaves everyone he knows, including his best friends. He tremendously enjoys their company. He gets to America and works like a dog just to survive. He then gets a better job opportunity and works his way up. He then opens his own company and works even harder. At sixty-five, he retires and goes back to his country. He meets up with his old friends, who are joking, drinking wine, and playing cards. It's been forty years since they have seen each other, so his friends are happy to see him but a little taken aback. He, on the other hand, takes this reunion with much more joyfulness. He explains to his friends how hard he had to work in order to come back to his country to live the rest of his life with his friends and do all the things they enjoy doing together. One of his friends stood up and simply said, "We have been doing this for the past forty years. Why did you leave?"

I don't know about you, but this story makes me think about what our society does. We work so long and hard, and for what? For bigger and better things, then we have less time for the things we love. In the end, we all get slapped with the same toe tag.

Shut My Cake Hole

A young woman was on my table, full of enthusiasm. She was talking nonstop from the start. I could barely get a word in. The topics she talked about went from *A* to *Z* in no time. It was difficult for me to keep up with her, so she did most of the talking in this eighty-minute massage.

She stated that people should really do what they love to do in life, and of course I strongly agreed. I mentioned that I massage a lot of young people who are going to college for reasons their parents wished for them and not what the child wishes for him- or herself.

I informed her that many young people shared with me that they are going to medical or law school because those are the wishes of their parents and not of themselves. I continued speaking on this topic until I began to think that she must have fallen asleep because she stopped talking.

Twenty minutes went by, and then I heard her utter the words, "My parents are both doctors."

"That's nice," I replied.

The next thing she said was, "I'm attending medical school," followed by crying and tears.

At this point, I felt that I'd said enough. I shut my cake hole and simply continued my massage and just tried to give her a safe space to deal with her thoughts.

This is the shit that happens to you when you live your life for others rather than for yourself!

I cannot emphasize enough how important it is to start thinking in terms of natural rather than normal. This young woman I just spoke of did the *normal* thing, which basically means what most people in our society would do. She went to medical school because both her parents were doctors. I'm going to go out on a limb here and assume that her parents planted the seed of medical school in their daughter's mind at a young age and continued to fertilize this seed into her young adulthood.

The *natural* approach to her issue would be to go off with her feelings, without the pressure, influence, or judgment of others.

This kind of thinking of normal and natural may be difficult at first, but I believe once you incorporate this kind of thinking into your life and continue to do so, it will seem as though you have been sleepwalking your whole life. As you become aware, you will notice that many people are still sleep-walking.

I too, just as this young woman, wanted to be normal. I wanted to be accepted by my peers, even if it meant doing what I did not enjoy. Their acceptance trumped my own happiness. This does not work as an adult, nor should it. Now I allow my own happiness to trump what others may think of me. I would only set myself up for failure if I didn't.

People who dance to the beat of their own drum, who are creative, and who come up with the newest inventions, solutions, and technology don't do so because they think like the rest of the people. They are successful because they *don't* think like the rest of the people. Smell that for a while!

4

GOAL VS. INTENTION

*If anyone on the verge of action
should judge himself according to the
outcome, he would never begin.*
—Kierkegaard

As a young teenager, the adults in my life would often ask me about my goals—what my goals were for the summer and even my distant future. I felt like telling them, "To get to the next grade." At that age, what else would have been my goal?

Then they would be spewing out the goals they accomplished. As if I cared. I guess that is what life is about, I thought.

If an adult were to ask me what intention was, I would have looked at him as if he were from another planet or if he thought I was hatching a scheme of some kind, like a bank job or a jewelry heist. The word *intention* was never in any kids' vocabulary.

The word *goal* was always associated with a good deed. The word *intention* was mainly associated with a negative event.

When I watched movies as a kid, the prosecuting attorney would always say something to the defendant on the stand like, "So your intention was to gain the trust of the family in order to ..." The television news would say, "The intention of the rapist was to ..." *Goal* was always used as a positive, and *intention* was always used as a negative. So why would I want or do anything that had to do with *intention?*

Well, our society got these two words mixed up too; however, I must say that these days it is being corrected. These days, *intention* is good, and *goals* are being used in a more negative way.

Webster's Dictionary states a *goal* as: "the place at which a race, trip, etc. is ended." It also states it as: "an end that one strives to attain."

Sound familiar to you? Most people are in a race. I don't know why or to where, but they are. Most people with a goal see the end ... but the end to what? They reach that end only to continue to strive for the next thing.

Webster's Dictionary states *intention* as "a purpose; a determination to act in a certain way; a reason why something is done."

It seems as if the words *goal* and *intention* are somewhat alike. But to me, they cannot be more opposite.

To me, *goal* is living in the future and *intention* is living in the present time.

When I started to live my life with more intentions and fewer goals, I found I needed to put out much less effort than before. I believe this kind of thinking is way overdue. We need to go back to the fundamentals and ask ourselves, *Why are we doing what we do?*

Ski Bunny

A thirtysomething investment banker on my table appeared very fit. She said she earned really good money, but for her it was just an okay job. While working, she would take every opportunity to fly out to Colorado to ski and be outdoors.

Goal vs. Intention

It got to the point where she realized that she needed to make this a bigger part of her life and not just long weekend trips. She decided to take EMT classes in order to work for the ski resorts in Colorado. This is what she truly wanted to do.

When she let her bosses and coworkers know *why* she was leaving her job, she expected them to try to knock some sense into her. What she didn't expect was the look of envy from them.

They were envious of her because she had the balls to give this all up for something that she loved to do. They, on the other hand, couldn't begin to imagine how to go about doing something like this and give up what they had.

But what exactly do they have? They have what I mentioned in chapter one—bigger and better everything—but now they feel stuck.

Only a few people can do what she did—trade her money for true happiness. She told me she absolutely never regretted the choice she made. It was her purpose/intention to live this kind of life.

This woman is a rare breed of people. I say this for a lot of reasons.

Now, and even growing up, I would notice and encounter people like her. There is something about these people that I can't put my finger on. I just know that they look and act different from most people.

These people seem confident but not cocky. They seem driven but very calm. When I come in contact with these people, they hold constant eye contact in a way that is not weird but rather comforting.

Now that I am older, I recognize and understand them

even more. The one trait these people have is that they are not influenced by the bullshit that society has bestowed upon them. The rest of us seem like sheep.

This woman, at her young age, lives her life with intention. This is someone who truly has her shit together. She does not need to impress other people.

Very often I hear people say that they live where they are because of their job but they would rather live somewhere else. They live close to family and relatives, but they are not living at their ideal place. I also hear that they put off where they truly want to live for when they retire, which does not make sense in many ways.

How the hell are you going to do all the things you enjoy doing when you're sixty-five? At age sixty-five, you may not be capable of doing things as you would in your thirties and forties. You simply might not be able to.

At sixty-five, you may be spending your time visiting doctors' offices and every kind of specialist out there.

People have too many *buts* in their lives. When you are young, wouldn't you want to live in a place you love and try to get work or create work there?

If you are an outdoor person and love the beach, mountains, sunny days, and snow, wouldn't you want a close drive to these places rather than long weekends of flying to Colorado from New York City, as that investment banker did at one time?

If you like art and culture, wouldn't you want to surround yourself with this lifestyle?

Goal vs. Intention

I think most people don't want to lose what they already have, even though they want better for themselves.

There came a point in my life when I realized that I was fighting hard not to give up my current lifestyle even though I wasn't crazy about it. I simply wasn't that happy. I wasn't sure why I was holding on so hard to this lifestyle. So I decided to give some kind of effort to a life that I truly wanted.

I guess some of us simply get comfortable or get used to how we live.

Let's break this goal-and-intention topic into its simplest form.

Let's say my *goal* was to live in California instead of New York. I would pack my car with lots of food and water so I stopped as little as possible in order to reach my goal as quickly as I could. As I am driving, I would be focused on staying on course and continue heading west. Before I know it, I'm there.

Now, if I was to go to California from New York with an *intention* rather than a goal, what would be my intention? Why do I want to go to California? It's not just to get from point *A* to point *B*. What do I exactly want from point *B* that I don't have from point *A*?

For me, the answer would be to live in a place with sunshine and nice climate, where I can spend more time outdoors. What does this do for me? For me, this translates to happiness.

So, when I begin my journey to California, I don't pack the car with food and water. I intentionally choose to stop where and when I want to. As I travel, I may end up driving off course, north or south, and stop in different towns or cities. I would take time to soak all these places in.

During my travels, I may discover there are *many* places besides California that I might consider to live instead—many places I didn't know much about that may offer sunshine, good climate, and outdoor activity, as well as or even better than California. The reason I would consider this is because I would be open to it.

Living with intention allows me to be open to other possibilities that may spark an interest as I travel through life.

Intentions Diet

There is always a new fad diet out there. I know people who have tried every diet possible and lose the weight and end up gaining it back, plus some. They have spent a lot of money and time in this process, and it's not pleasant to be around them, especially if it happens to be a spouse or someone you live with. Of course, they act like happy-go-lucky to the outside world, but not so much at home.

These diet books give you all the information about the calories, protein, nutrients, and vitamins that each freakin' berry, seed, or green bean has. It even tells you what damn time to eat them. These diet programs make you so food knowledgeable. It makes you eager to go over other peoples' houses who are also on a diet so you both pontificate on the merits of certain vegetables.

I would often open one of these books, not because I was starting a diet, but just to look. What a bore! Nobody gets whacked, and it lacks drama. Can't they at least have a plot of some kind? Perhaps how strawberries have a tendency to undermine raspberries. All kidding aside, these books are missing the most important element—*intention*!

The focus should not be on losing weight. The focus should be on why you want to be healthy, why you want to be fit, why you want to lose those extra pounds that cause health problems, why you want a clear and sharp mind, and why you want to feel like you can go up and down stairs with ease and be able to run a half-marathon at will.

For heaven's sake, why would anyone in his right mind not want to live such a healthy and vigorous life?

Intention needs to be established on any matter if you expect transformation.

My intention for my diet is quite simple. So what is my intention? My intention is what I just stated earlier.

My intention is not to go on a diet. It is to feel fit, not carry extra weight, and for my mind to be more clear and efficient.

So how do I *let go* of this needless weight? Keep in mind, I used *let go* instead of *lose*. Nobody wants to *lose* anything—from car keys to jobs. But you do want to *let go* of things in your life whenever it is the right time. For example, you *let go* of your car keys when you need to upgrade, and you *let go* of your current job for a better job. It is a psychological thing. *Lose* is a word that has a negative connotation. *Let go* is more positive and motivating.

So what would my *eating habits* be? Again, I don't call it a diet. I'd rather call it *eating habits*. My habit would be to consume less portions and eat smarter. Let's get real. I think we basically know the good food from the crap. This kind of eating habit is relatively small, but the results are big.

This eating habit started with an intention, which was to feel healthier and think clearer.

How Not to Become an Actor

As I stated earlier, the emotions I saw in films planted a seed in my head. As a kid, I grew up *being seen and not heard*. I was holding all my emotions inside. I never expressed them. I so badly wanted to vomit my emotions out like Linda Blair in *The Exorcist*. But I couldn't. At least not at that age. This acting seed remained dormant until I was in my early twenties. I decided it was a good time to pursue acting.

I had no intention whatsoever; however, I had a goal. I had a goal that was significantly pointless. I decided to try to get into the acting business via a position as a props person, a grip, basically anything within ten feet of the acting itself. "Brilliant," I thought. "Let me bust my hump to get these positions rather than taking the proper acting classes or some kind of training." So there I go, sneaking into the filming of a Woody Allen movie and getting to know his key grip so I can learn to be a grip myself. I was trying to get from point *A* to point *B* on the longest, hardest, most tiring route possible. This was not getting me closer to my goal of becoming an actor.

So I decided to do it on my own. I got a headshot and résumé and started to hit the streets of New York City with more passion than Joe Buck in the movie *Midnight Cowboy*.

With no agent and even less training and talent, all my auditions were open calls from *The Backstage*, a newspa-

Goal vs. Intention

per that actors used when they had no one to represent them.

I went on many auditions and got no gigs. I would hear a lot of thank-you's, which meant "Get the hell out of my face." I also got a lot of advice, like "You may want to get some training before you consider auditioning again." At one of my last auditions, the casting director said, "We know you can read. But can you act out what you read?" That was how bad I was. At this point in my life, I had great stamina. I was as strong as an ox and almost as smart. I came to the realization that I had to have at least some talent if I was going to work as an actor. So I decided to hold off on my auditions until I had some form of training, which I eventually got.

After the training, I heard different feedback. I heard things like, "Do it again, but change this part," or "Let's see you do it a bit differently, with a twist." I would get callbacks, and eventually I did get some gigs. Once I built up my confidence, I got very good gigs. The bizarre part of this is that I never considered myself an actor until I started making money from acting.

When I first began trying to be an actor, I worked for free, and it was fun. But still, I never considered myself an actor. It took freakin' paychecks to validate what I was doing. The critical part of my brain would only believe it when the artistic side of my brain earned money. Then when a gig paid too little, I didn't even want to audition for it. The more money I received, the better actor I thought I was. Those paychecks were building up my ego and diminishing my acting abilities gradually.

I lost my purpose for why I started acting, which was

to express myself, to show emotions, to *feel* at will. Once I got a lot of money, it was as though subconsciously all I ever wanted was to make money at it. I didn't want to feel or show anything to anyone anymore. I felt "done." In this case, I guess I lost my *intention* and my *goal* to act. I'm still trying to figure this one out.

In order for the pain to go away, I had to make light of the situation. I had to convince myself that acting was my backup plan if massage therapy did not work out.

Mirror, Mirror on the Wall

Most people's lives remain largely unexamined by the most important person in their lives—*themselves.*

I find it amazing how differently I look at situations depending on where I am in my life as I mature. A great example is a film by Martin Scorsese called *Raging Bull* with Robert De Niro. When I first saw the movie at the age of twenty, I thought it was a great film about boxing. Ten years later when I watched it again, I concluded that this film has nothing to do with boxing; it is a film about a guy who doesn't know how to get along with other people in his life. Ten years went by, and after seeing it again, I concluded that this is a film about a guy who can't even live in his own skin.

This is a film I've seen throughout my life, and the meaning changed numerous times for me. This movie has nothing to do with boxing. Currently, now that I'm in my fifties, I believe it's about learning to accept and get along with yourself, and then getting along with others is a walk in the park.

Goal vs. Intention

I am hesitant to view this film again only because at this point in my life I may think this is a great movie about boxing again. That would not be a good sign.

Looking at myself in the mirror and reflecting is something I enjoy and something that is very helpful, especially when I bring my shaving equipment along.

Talking to yourself in the mirror is very therapeutic. I ask myself meaningful questions. I then pause to collect my thoughts and answer myself back. If you ask an honest question, you will get an honest answer. Think about it. You can't lie to yourself. You know when someone is lying to you, especially when it's yourself that is doing the lying. If it's good enough for Robert De Niro in *Taxi Driver*, then it is good enough for me.

Just for laughs, try lying to yourself while staring into a mirror. It is not easy. You could get away with lying to yourself while you are having a conversation in your own head, however while in the mirror and making eye contact with yourself…not easy at all. If this comes easy to you, there may be a slight chance you are *crackers*.

On a side note, since I'm on the topic of Robert De Niro movies, I'd like to share a story of three separate encounters I had with him. I was working security at the Plaza Hotel in New York City in the late '80s, and he was about to hold a press conference for his new movie, *Midnight Run*, that was just about to be released.

One of his people approached me and gave me very specific orders. "Robert De Niro is going to walk through that revolving door. I want you to inform yourself to him and escort him to the elevator. I want you to make sure no one else enters that elevator and key the elevator so it doesn't stop until it gets to the seventeenth floor. While in the elevator, under no circumstances will you offer to shake his hand, start a conversation, or even make eye contact."

That was thirty years ago, and I remember every word that came out of this guy's mouth because that is how much I admired Robert De Niro back then. I've encountered many celebrities at the Plaza Hotel but was never star struck, except when I saw "Bobby." I did try to make eye contact in the elevator with him, but he was too focused on the elevator floor, as though he was staring at a dime and trying to make heads or tails out of it.

A few months later, I was in the streets of NYC using a pay phone to talk to my girlfriend, Linda, who is now my wife. I spotted Robert De Niro walking down the street, heading toward me. As he got closer, I told my wife that Robert De Niro was walking toward me, but she didn't care at all, only because she was never star struck and never will be.

He stopped before me and used the pay phone right next to me. I couldn't believe it. This was my chance to meet him and not worry about getting fired from the Plaza. I whispered to Linda, "You're not gonna believe this. Robert De Niro is using the pay phone right next to me."

She responded, "What time will you be home?" That's how star struck she is not. As I was rehearsing what I was going to say to him in my head, he quickly hung up and walked away just as fast. I lost my chance.

Now for the sake of time, this encounter I just wrote about happened again a few months later—only it was a different part of New York City, but still while talking to my girlfriend, Linda, and again with her asking when I

Goal vs. Intention

would be home after telling her Robert De Niro was using the pay phone next to me again.

So now, back to the mirror. I had to get to know and understand myself in order to know what my intention was in life. I wanted to live with a purpose. But how do I even begin? Where do I start?

I made myself a résumé. It wasn't a résumé for a job. It was a résumé for my life. I didn't know myself very well. So I had to put it on paper. I know what you're thinking; I must be bonkers. Maybe I am.

However, I noticed throughout my life that whenever someone I just met would ask me to tell them about myself, I never had a good answer. If I did, it would take a lot of research on my part. I also noticed that when someone would ask me to describe a friend or coworker to them, I would have no problem doing so, and I would also be very precise when describing them. How the hell is this possible? I've been living with myself my whole life and cannot describe myself to anyone.

So I snapped into action and wrote a life résumé for myself. I wasn't looking for a job. I was looking for a better understanding of myself and what makes me tick. My life résumé is far more important than any job résumé.

The purpose of this résumé is not so I can answer a stranger asking about my life. It is so I can be very clear about my intention, purpose, and beliefs (and I don't mean religious beliefs). It contained what kind of relationships I want and what I really enjoy doing. Once you are clear about what you want out of life, then choices in your life will come easier to you because you understand not only who you are but what floats your boat.

This is similar to a vision board that many people make, and I think that's great. I had one too, but it did not work for me, and I know why. I never knew where to start. It was overwhelming and looked like a Picasso painting when he'd been drinking. So I took it down and only kept the picture of what I wanted and laid it flat on my dresser. The rest of the vision board stayed in my closet. That picture, and only that picture, is what I focused on. Once I did, what I desired came to me very quickly.

Case in point, for a very long time, I wanted a dog, particularly a boxer. So I put a picture of a boxer on my dresser. Let me explain something. My wife did not want a dog in the house. The chance of a fancy sports car or a yacht were much greater at this point than having a dog in my house. But the dog is what I wanted more at this time than anything else in my life.

I would look at the picture of this boxer, and I would imagine playing with it. I would feel all the emotions of having this dog. I would even imagine cleaning up the crap.

I went ahead and got this boxer after a short time, without my wife's blessing. The cliché that it is easier to ask for forgiveness than it is for permission is true! I felt the emotions of what I wanted, focusing on one thing only, and it manifested very quickly. If I had the vision board up and tried to feel the emotions of fifty different things, it would have been impossible. I find that the universe will respond very quickly when you focus and feel one thing at a time.

In case you are wondering about the rest of my vision board, it turns out I no longer needed those pictures. I no longer wanted those things. No interest whatsoever. You see, I did such a great job imagining my feelings and

Goal vs. Intention

emotions with some items on my board that I no longer had to have them because my imagination and feelings toward them was sometimes enough.

To me, a thought of the future is the same as a memory from the past. *They don't exist.* This kind of thinking will take you places or not take you places. Whatever you prefer. Let me explain. My wife wants to travel. Me, not so much. I did enough traveling when I worked for the airlines.

These days with the clarity (high-definition) of television there is no reason to visit Paris or any other place. I can simply put on a DVD that shows the streets, parks, buildings, museums, beaches, etc., of the place I want to visit. I sit on my couch with fine cheese and wine and feel all the emotions I would experience if I were there.

I also would not have to deal with the traffic, renting a car, parking a car, waiting in lines, and all the shit that sucks about vacations. But mostly the crowds. Don't get me wrong. I like people. I just think there are too many of them.

East Is Best! West Is Best!

I have lived most of my life in the eastern parts of the United States. I now live in the Southwest. I've also visited many places in the East and the West. I found that there are significant differences in the attitudes of the people in each place.

In the east, life seems to be about the present and the past. Out west, it's about the present and the future.

What I mean is that people in the east are very structured and set in their ways. Their attitude is, "This is who my parents were. This is who I am, and this is who my kids will be." They mainly focus on their goals with blinders on and reach their goals fairly quickly.

When I say people out west are about the present and the future, it's because their attitude is, "This is who I am now, and we will see what tomorrow brings." They are open to the future.

The more open you are in life, the more doors you will find open along the way. If you are too focused on that distinct door, you will not see other doors that may suddenly start to open for you.

Once I was able to distinguish between goal and intention, it took a lot of stress off me. I realized that living with intention is easy and effortless. It is easier to *be* rather than to *do*. I still have goals in my life. At least that's how they start. When I transform those goals with the thought of intention, I find myself not striving for anything anymore. I simply start to live for the purpose of how that goal started.

These days the only goals I have are mainly on my to-do list, which I place in front of my coffeemaker so I see it in the morning. These goals are the ones I cross off my list when completed.

I can cross off my *goals*, but it is difficult to cross off an intention. It is possible, and there are times when I may want to cross off one of my intentions, but that would mean a change or modification on a belief I had, and that's okay.

I like to think about having a "to-be" list. By adding an adjective next to some of your to-do list goals, you will have created a to-be list as well. For example, if on your list, you have "Call Bill about the issue at work," you can add "be understanding," or "be patient," or "be calm." Be mindful

Goal vs. Intention

to choose the proper adjective next to your list of to-dos. For example, it's better to write "mow the lawn proudly" rather than "mow the lawn victoriously." Otherwise your neighbors may call the nice men with the nice white jackets to come take you away. I won't go any further, but I will tell you that when I add a to-be to my list, it makes it more enjoyable.

5

YOUR BELIEFS WILL CARRY YOU

*True wisdom comes to each of
us when we realize how little we
understand about life, ourselves, and
the world around us.*
—*Socrates*

The message I want to convey is not to put all your trust on information handed down to you. If you think about it, most of what we believe is not from our own experience but from other people's experiences—parents, relatives, friends, and the media.

There are many theories out there but very few facts. Theories will always change as we grow, evolve, and progress. In my lifetime alone, theories about various topics have changed back and forth many times over. The foods thought to be good for you back then are now bad. And with time, these same foods will be claimed as good for you again.

Pluto was discovered to be a planet, only to be discovered that it is no longer a planet, then rediscovered to be a planet.

Scientists and media have a clever way of covering up a mistake. They phrase it as "New studies show ..." Holy crap! How brilliant is that? Nobody looks like a fool. Imagine if we were all to use this phrase at our workplace, in our relationships, and in our daily lives. Imagine coming home to your spouse after you had a big fight and simply saying, "Honey, new studies show that you are not an ass." Imagine telling your boss after you screwed up that new studies show ... So why stress about who is right and who is wrong? It is all what you believe at that time, and with more time it may reverse itself. Not much of life is permanent. So you and the person you have a conflict with may both be right, but no one has the final answer because neither of you know the true answer.

Childhood Beliefs

As a kid, I believed in Santa Claus just like any other kid my age would because of the information given to me by adults. I was told of the long journey Santa had ahead of him and how he visited all the kids' houses, dropping off presents.

When my oldest son was five years old, he stopped believing in Santa Claus on his own. When I asked him why, his response was, "No one can go all over the world and deliver all these presents in one night."

His answer made me feel like a fool because I, myself, believed in Santa Claus until I was twice his age—as do many other children. I was told the truth by my older friends. I never put two and two together. As a kid living in Brooklyn, I knew it took at least fifteen minutes for my mom to get bread and milk from the corner store. How could I have been so ignorant? I was bamboozled my whole young life by this Santa Claus story. To keep this Santa story in perspective, we still get bamboozled in our teens, at midlife, and even as we get older. But this time it's by the media, news, advertisers, and social standards that we think we have to follow.

As an adult, if someone were to sit down and watch the news and hear politicians say, "This government is too big," the next day around the water cooler, everyone else would begin to say the same thing, and with time, that is all we would talk about. It becomes a very big topic, and people want to know how to fix this issue.

So what are we comparing this fact about our government being too big with? Compared to most developed countries, our government is not too big. Anything that is discussed in the news and then spoken about by people will snowball to the point where it will become our primary focus.

This is how wars start. We, as Americans, do not want war and will avoid it at all costs, unless the government and the news convinces us that there may be no other choice. They do this by instilling fear into us. Once they put enough fear into us, we will even agree to go to war with our own neighbors.

I'm not saying that you have to research everything yourself. You will not have enough hours in the day to do so. I just think we need to be more selective about how we perceive the information we receive and not have a knee-jerk reaction to what we hear. Anything we focus on will only get bigger, stronger, and grow faster. If the internet was around when I was five years old, I would have Googled this Santa Claus character.

Religion

I was raised in a Catholic family, so naturally that was my belief. I thought I had to keep the same religion as my family so it would be passed on from generation to generation. That was all I knew.

Right after attending the christening of my daughter,

one of my friends, who was not Catholic, approached my wife and I and expressed how scary that ritual was for her. "What are you talking about?" I looked at her with confusion.

"What the priest said was scary," she replied. Still confused, I asked her if she could repeat some of what the priest had said. So she did. Out of her mouth were lines that sounded like they were taken from the movie *The Exorcist*. She quoted lines such as *cleanse her from her sins; withstand the devil;* and *denounce the devil*. When I viewed the video of the christening the next day, I kept an open mind and listened carefully to every word the priest had said. Indeed, it was a bit scary.

I grew up going to church as a kid, but it all sounded the same to me. So I tuned it out. Even as an adult, I tuned it out. I would physically show up, but my mind would be elsewhere. For me, it sounded like the adults in the *Charlie Brown* cartoon—wah-wah-wah-wah-wah.

My daughter's christening did not change my religion at that time; however, this was the start to my becoming more aware.

It wasn't until my older son was taking religion classes in order to receive his first Holy Communion that we finally ended our association with the Catholic religion. While my son was attending these *catechism* classes, my wife said that right before each class, my son was on the floor, crying while curled up in a ball as if he was in pain. He was saying, "I don't want to go to that class! I feel like I'm bad!" We decided to bring him to a counselor. The counselor informed us that our son feels bad about himself while attending class. He told her that he tries to be a good kid every week, and every week they make him stand up in class and tell the class the bad things he did that week.

Holy crap! I thought.

I started looking back into my younger years and realized that I felt the very same way back then. However, if I ever told my parents that, it wouldn't have gone over as well.

I saw myself as that kid again, living my life with constant shame and guilt. I couldn't live a natural life. I felt like I was being judged even if I was in a room by myself because the God I knew was constantly judging me. I thought I could never make him happy. It was as if he was just waiting for my next wrong move, or even a wrong thought. I was very unhappy. I accepted this feeling as being normal. It sucked. This was my belief, as it was my world.

I realized in later years that life is not painful nor should it be. Not living your life is what is painful. I had to learn to forgive myself for any wrongdoing I thought I did at that time.

Guilt and self-judgment does not necessarily have a time frame. Unlike someone who commits a crime and serves a sentence. Once he serves his sentence, he is free of the crime he committed. So why did I have such a problem forgiving myself for something that never even landed me in jail, or even close to it? Why did I hang on to these feelings? I now know that I was treating myself as if I was continually serving a jail sentence when I didn't have to.

I have said many dumb things in my life, and I know that I will continue to do so, but hopefully not nearly as much. But I made it a point to forgive myself in advance. I'm doing the best I can and will not hurt anyone's feelings intentionally.

Many people grew up with the belief that they were stupid. Many of these people still believe that. I can't imagine a little kid having that kind of thought about himself unless it was planted by an adult. Some of these same kids grew up believing that they were not loved. They were criticized and shamed—a true recipe for anger and violence. Any of us, under certain conditions, could end up in jail.

I, you, or anyone else is capable of theft, abuse, violent crimes, and even murder. Yes, I said murder. The reason you didn't commit any of these crimes is because you were lucky enough not to be put in a situation that would lead you to do this. I'm not talking about shooting someone because of road rage. That's just plain stupidity. Road rage happens because if someone cuts you off, you will never see them again, and this is the only time in your life that you can get back at them. Like I said, that is just stupidity. These are grown-up kids who will carry their beliefs of stupidity to their graves. When someone cuts me off, I just let it go. I am in a better place than they are at the time.

Another difference between you and a criminal is that you have a better capability of keeping your life in order. This could be because of your upbringing and education.

Judgment Day

I saw something recently on the news that is worth sharing. There was a female judge sentencing a man who committed burglary. The television showed a split-screen. The judge was on the left side. She seemed like a no-nonsense kind of judge. On the right side of the screen was the accused man.

After the judge gave him his guilty sentence, she said, I want to ask you a question. Did you go to *XYZ* middle school?" The criminal stared at her and realized that they were friends in middle school. He could not believe it was her and started to show a great deal of emotion and cried continuously as the cameras continued to roll. The judge stated to the courtroom that this man was the nicest kid in the class and that she always wondered what happened to him. This was very emotional for me to watch.

So what prevents you and I from burglarizing homes? I believe we are lucky enough not to be in his exact situation. This same man in front of my own eyes no longer looked like a criminal. He looked like a man who did a bad thing for which he was very sorry and ashamed of. I saw this adult man on my TV screen, and as he got emotional, I wondered how his beliefs were formed and at what point in his life things went wrong.

Shirley Temple

We would all live our lives with unlimited potential if we decided to let go of the negative beliefs we learned as we were growing up. Imagine that everything that we attempted came without criticism. The fear of making fools of ourselves would almost certainly guarantee that it would happen. Letting go of that criticism is what will allow you to be the best you can at any endeavor.

Shirley Temple was four years old when she started

acting, singing, and dancing. Acting came effortlessly to her. Of course, she had to practice her singing and had to practice even more when she was dancing. I don't think she climbed down from her crib just knowing how to dance like that. But generally, I truly believe some people can be naturals when it comes to acting.

Shirley Temple's career didn't last long. The same is true for most other child actors. Most of these very young children were never asked to act in front of the camera. They instead were asked to *be*. At four years old, they don't really know what acting is. At that age, they can't distinguish good acting from bad acting.

So why do these kids' careers end as they get older? As a young child, they don't know criticism. They don't even know the meaning of this dreadful word yet. But eventually they grow, and as they do, criticism from others can place an invisible barrier between themselves and all their hopes and dreams.

Let's think about this for a while. It's much more fun when they're not being judged. Once they begin to feel judged, they don't act as well and don't enjoy it as well either.

When we were raising our older son, he was on a soccer team. The boys on the team were very young, and they enjoyed playing soccer. The parents on the sidelines also enjoyed watching their kids playing and having fun. It didn't matter if their team won or lost. It didn't even matter if a boy accidentally happened to kick the ball in his own goal. All the boys got equal time on the field. It was fun for all—the boys, parents, and coaches.

However, what a difference a couple of months made.

After that season, a new one started shortly. The boys were on exactly the same teams. They had the exact same parents, and they had the exact same coaches as last time. What the fuck happened in the couple of months in between? I don't know. But there was a sudden shift in the attitudes of the coaches and parents. They were much harder on their boys. They expected much more from them than before. I believe these boys began to feel judged and criticized for their performance by their coaches and parents. Hence, the word "performance." The boys now knew who the better players were. Even equal amount of play time was nonexistent. The "good" players played, and the others were on the sidelines pulling blades of grass. I'm sure that these boys' beliefs about themselves were affected by this. Since the tension grew stronger with each game, my wife and I, along with our son, decided not to continue with soccer.

Wouldn't it be nice to do things without performing? Some of us are so accustomed to judgment that we don't even need to be in the presence of people to feel judged. We've conditioned ourselves to judge ourselves. We don't sing in the shower or dance alone in an empty room to great music—something that is very therapeutic to do. So, for crying out loud, sing and dance all you want!

Wasted Talent

I was in an acting class many years ago with another student who was a brilliant actor. All his peers thought so too, including the teacher. While I knew him, he never got any acting gigs. His belief was that he couldn't go on auditions because he wasn't *ready*.

Every week before class, other actors would mention to the class what gigs they got. These are the same actors who were fair at best but managed to get work because they hustled, took chances, and were resilient. That's just about 90 percent of what you need to be an actor. The other 10 percent is the talent itself.

We were all unsure of what this talented actor was waiting for. I'm not putting this guy down, but that was wasted talent. He never took that first step needed to pursue his dreams and share his talent.

Our beliefs are fluid. In my case, I change my beliefs based on my new experiences. I like to believe this is progress for me. If I were to think I know it all, then I would wake up to a new day with nothing to learn. And nothing is what I would learn.

I learned that Santa Claus was fake. I learned that religion of any kind was not good for me. I learned that I was not stupid. I now create my beliefs from my own experiences and encourage others to do the same.

Worry Backpack: BAD
Hopeful Backpack: GOOD

As far back as I can remember, I was a worrier. I thought I had to worry in order to survive in this life. My mother was a worrier. Perhaps I got it from her. It wasn't until much later in my life that I realized that worrying was ruining my life and creating a lot of unhappiness. I had this false belief that if I worried enough about everything there is to worry about, then when that bad event actually happened, I would be prepared for it. Yup! That was exactly my strategy. As you can guess, it wasn't a good strategy.

It was like going about my day carrying a backpack full of worries. This backpack would get heavier as time went on because I kept filling it up, getting ready for emergency situations. When a bad event would happen, I would reach into my heavy backpack and pull out something that I thought would help me out, but instead, I pulled out a lot of shit that I'd been carrying all my life for no good reason.

None of these worries in my backpack ever helped me. They only weighed me down. I would say that almost all these worries I carried with me never came true. It was all in my head, and that was all.

So I decided to try the opposite. I got a new backpack and filled it with good thoughts rather than bad ones. I started to think that maybe I would win the lottery or a raffle. (Mind you, I don't play the lottery, and I never enter any raffles.) I would also think things like, Maybe I will find a hundred-dollar bill on the floor. Maybe I will see an old friend on the street and have coffee with him. Maybe I will get a raise or a promotion. Only good thoughts would go in my backpack. Now, let me tell you this. The chances of those good things happening are just as slim as the bad thoughts I was worrying about.

So what is the advantage of carrying good thoughts in my backpack, even though they may not come true? There are many answers to this. Carrying that backpack with worries got heavier and heavier and continually weighed me down. I looked at life while just waiting for the bad shit to happen. You could even see it in my eyes, if you knew me.

When I put good stuff in my backpack, I would feel lighter and lighter each day. I would look forward to life and all its possibilities. I was full of hope. My attitude was better among people. My energy was better. I would bet money that if you walked around with a hopeful backpack rather than one that is full of shit, you would be a much happier person and your energy would change to the positive, just like it did for me. I walked around with a much better attitude. It gave me a fresh outlook on life, and it showed. I feel safe to say that given these two scenarios, opportunities will come easier to someone with a good attitude. Smell that for a while.

Round-Tailed Ground Squirrel

I was on the way to work at the resort one day. It was an average day, just like any other. As I was walking, I stopped and noticed a little round-tailed ground squirrel just staring at me from a distance. As I got closer, I noticed he was not moving out of my way. I then slowed up my walking pace, and he started to come toward me. I tried to stay calm while I continued to walk.

As he got about three feet from me, I stopped walking and stood as still as I could. He also stood still. I made eye contact with this squirrel, and he proceeded to walk toward me and climbed up on my foot. He stood there just staring at me. I sensed he was not threatened by me because of the length of time he stood on my foot. A sense of calm came over me. I felt at peace with this tiny creature and with the

Your Beliefs Will Carry You

nature all around me. I slowly began walking again, and he peacefully climbed down my foot.

When I got to my workplace, I entered the break room, where all the other massage therapists hung out. I felt so special. I was filled with peace and joy, as if I was one with my surroundings. I did not share what just happened with any of my coworkers because from my experience, when someone brags how humble or spiritual they are, it only means they wish they were.

During that day and a few days after the encounter with this little creature, I noticed I felt connected with everyone around me in a more sincere and spiritual way. I had a deeper understanding of my clients, and I even gave better massages. My interactions with them were more meaningful. This small creature further enforced my purpose in life, which is to love and be loved for who I am.

A week went by, and I was in the breakroom, hanging out with other therapists. The conversation was about the local wildlife in this area. So I figured this would be a good time to share my experience about that little squirrel. I wasn't bragging. I just told my story as any other peaceful, humble, and spiritual man would have.

In that breakroom was a coworker of mine—someone very judgmental, negative, almost always full of anger, and not liked by anyone there. After telling my story, out of this person's mouth came this: "Oh yeah. That squirrel did the same thing to me. That squirrel does that to everyone. Everyone feeds that squirrel. That's why he comes to us."

It was at this time that my hopes for delivering life wisdom to all those around me collapsed like a house of cards, and what a slow, steady wind it was that took that house down. I witnessed the very last cards slowly crumbling down.

This little freakin' creature had me believing that I was a beacon of light. That following week at work, I felt like a complete fraud. I was worried that those clients I massaged while I was in *Zen squirrel zone* would sense my fakeness and would see me as a schmuck-on-wheels.

Do you see how the strength of our beliefs can alter us as a person? Can you see how powerful beliefs can change our life? Can you see them as beliefs and merely beliefs? For one full week, this squirrel had me changing my beliefs about myself and life. I felt like a fraud for only a couple of days afterward. Then I said to myself, "Screw it! I will not have what that negative coworker said affect the good feelings I was having. I will just continue as if I were a humble, spiritual, Zen person."

I'm glad that I met that little bastard. It proved to me that my beliefs can change my world.

6

THE GREAT DIRECTOR

Where am I?
Who am I?
How did I come to be here?
What is this thing called the world?
How did I come into the world?
Why was I not consulted?
And if I am compelled to take part in
it, where is the director?
I want to see him!
—Kierkegaard

The greatest director you will ever know in your lifetime is yourself. Your life is like a movie. No one except you can create the kind of films that you can. Sometimes you create these films from all the thoughts and beliefs you think as you live your life. Many of these thoughts are false and negative, and you believe them. And if you continue to believe them, you will be producing the same negative films over and over and over again.

If there are any missing pieces in the puzzle of your day, you tend to fill in these blanks with your distorted truths, ideas, and imagination simply because you have to before you put your head on that pillow.

Before I go any further, I encourage you to stop and think and come to an awareness. You can change the thoughts, beliefs, and experiences you've had in the past by using fresh eyes (lenses).

I was so excited about this thought of mine that it felt destined to become a poem. However, this poem does lack rhythmical, metaphorical, and aesthetical qualities:

You have no camera, crew, or screen. You show people your films through your attitude and behavior. You are good at reaching your target audience. You know exactly who to show your films to and who not to show them to. Those who don't like your films tend not to enter your theater. Some will show up simply out of sympathy, but they would rather be in a different theater. As time passes, you may come to realize that your films are your life's thoughts. Perhaps your audience dwindles down with time. They may get tired of your films, or they may outgrow your films because now they are past that. Now you realize you need fresh faces for your films and that you need to be more selective. Or maybe, just maybe, you yourself will come to a realization that you need to produce better films.

I had to change my films. At an early age, I knew I had to. I got to the point where I didn't even want to see my own work. I started hanging out with different directors. Some specialized in drama, some in action and adventure, some in documentaries—all of whom I was familiar with. But I soon discovered a genre of movie that I was not familiar with. It was comedy.

As a kid, I watched *Abbott and Costello* and *The Three Stooges*, but I didn't know how to incorporate that kind of comedy in my life. There was no place for it. I simply couldn't find myself hitting someone over the head with a sledgehammer.

I must have been about twelve years old when I became friends with this young director who was also my age. He made me laugh. It felt good to be in his presence. I enjoyed every minute we spent together, and I couldn't get enough. His work as a director was something I had never seen before, and I wanted so badly to learn from him. I wanted to get in his head.

I remember vividly the first time he was at my house (main theater). When he left, my mom asked me, "What's wrong with him?" I looked at her and wondered if she saw something I may have missed.

"What do you mean?" I asked. I looked at her puzzlingly.

She responded by saying, "Why is he so happy?" That is when I realized the kind of theater I was living in. I knew then and there that if I wanted to make good films for the remainder of my life, I had a lot of work to do, and I needed to get started yesterday. The theater I grew up with was not familiar with these kinds of films that my comedic friend produced. I did not know such films even existed. I also realized that the films I was making in the past were not conducive to the lifestyle I now wanted. I had to incorporate my friend's work into my films.

Only when I incorporated comedy into my already-existing films did I realize that my work wasn't so bad after all. My work was simply lacking a substance so paramount that no film career could ever flourish without the existence of comedy. To this day, I still try to make the best films possible. It may not be easy for everyone because of certain circumstances in their lives, but it's best if they try and never give up.

How Right She Is

I went to greet a client in the waiting area who must have been in her eighties. She had a full head of pure-white, fluffy hair. I assumed she was in pretty good shape because of how easily she seemed to get around. She still had a spring in her step. And boy, was she a talker! As always, I don't talk to clients during their massage unless they want to … and believe me; she wanted to. The conversation was not deep at all—only small talk—the kind I could do without.

Halfway through our session, I pointed out that she was

more full of life than most young people I knew. She then told me a story that I will never forget.

One of her two daughters, who was twenty years old at the time, was killed by a drunk driver. With compassion, I said, "I'm so sorry." After a slight pause, I added, "I can't imagine how I could ever go on living if one of my children passed away." But the thought in my head at the time was, What's wrong with this woman? How can she be so happy? Why is she so full of life if her daughter got killed by a drunk driver?

She continued to say that when her daughter died, it was a living hell for herself, her husband, and her other daughter. For years, her family was miserable and could not find anything to smile about in this unfair world. She told me it got to the point where the spirits of the remaining members of her family also died. Their bodies were still pumping blood, but that was all. In spirit, they were dead. She said they might as well have been buried themselves. They believed they had no choice but just to exist.

One day she called a meeting with her family. They needed to make a choice. There were only two choices. The first choice was to continue to live like they had been since the death of their loved one. The other choice was to live their lives as they did before her death. They chose the latter.

They did not forget her death and never would. They decided it was not fair or right to have their other daughter's life also taken away because of this, which was exactly what had been happening.

There are not very many times during my massages that I shed a tear. This was indeed a time.

Even though I am one who speaks and writes about living a joyful life, I find myself ashamed of what I was thinking. I knew that I could never be as brave and optimistic as this woman was if that were to happen to me—not in a million years.

This woman had a fatal tragedy in her real life's film and somehow had the will and courage to change her outlook for the benefit of the remaining life of her family. We all have the power to do this. We just have to realize it.

Traveling Film Festivals

We are traveling film festivals for the world to see. We take our films everywhere we go. We even take our films with us when we move to different locations. We desire to create new movies, better movies, and happier movies with better endings. This plan sounds great, but when we move to new locations, we also bring with us the same director.

When we move to a new place, we have the same director we had before, but the scenery and background have changed. So the films are now made in a new location, but the type of production will not change unless the director, him- or herself transforms.

There may be situations where the director cannot produce the films he/she really wants because of the crew (people he/she surrounds him- or herself with). This is the kind of crew he/she is familiar with. He/She may come to an awareness that he/she needs to find a crew that is conducive to his/her life if he/she wants to create the films he/she truly wants.

I like to play *Director Game*. I came up with this because I wanted to detach myself from situations where I find myself too emotionally involved.

I imagine a situation where things are so difficult and so emotionally draining that I no longer could think rationally. Once I get to that point, I yell, "Cut!" I don't lose sight of the stage. I make my way to the balcony and sit because I want to distance myself from the characters and their emotions. I now replace the existing actors with new ones. The most important actor to replace is myself. I do not replace the actors with anyone you know. I just use stock actors. Keep in mind, that they are all in the same situation and same script and have the same motive.

I am no longer a player now. Just an observer. I can now think clearly and objectively. This is just a game I play. Once I became a professional in this game, it became how I naturally started thinking.

One man on my table informed me that he was in a very stressful situation at work and it was really getting to him. Ironically, as I tried to explain the *Director Game* to him, his response was, "I am a director, and I'm stressing about the movie I am making." He was having issues with the actors he was working with. This particular director started his career directing commercials. Now he directed films. Directing commercials and films are very different for many reasons.

Commercial actors are typically not famous. They are grateful to be working and take direction very well. Now this director is working with well-known actors who have been around for a while, along with their egos (no explanation necessary).

Mel Brooks

I recently did a house call with an older woman whose husband passed away a year earlier. She missed him dearly. This fact was very evident. Not only were her walls full of her husband's photos, but she also had lit candles in front of the photos of him set on various tables throughout the room. One of them was directly facing me while I was massaging her, and I ended up staring at him longer than I needed to. I felt like I knew him, and I wished he was still there for her.

Her mind was still greatly consumed with his passing. She shared something that was very bothersome to her. Years before her husband's death, she attended a party with him. A woman her husband knew approached them. During the conversation, this other woman said something that really upset this client of mine. She did not share what it was, and I did not ask her, nor did I need to know. But whatever it was, she was very upset about it. She mentioned that a day did not go by that she didn't think about this woman's statement.

I encouraged her to play a game with this situation that was making her so distraught. I suggested that she imagine that same scene between the three of them as if a movie was being filmed, only this time, to turn this movie from a drama into a comedy.

I asked her to take the same lines that the other woman told them, which were making her so angry, into a comedy movie directed by Mel Brooks, Rob Reiner, or Harold Ramis. She let me know that she likes Mel Brooks, so I told her to go with him as her choice. I asked her to imagine that just before that woman approached her and her husband that Mel Brooks was coaching the other woman on how to say that line. The script itself did not change one iota, nor did the background nor props. Only the director was replaced.

I could tell by the expression on her face that she was not open to what I was asking her to do. I persuaded her to give it a try. Two weeks later when I arrived at her house for her massage, she was very enthusiastic to let me know how well that game of mine had been working out for her. She told me that now when she thinks back at what that woman told them at the party, she laughs. She was able to laugh simply because she changed that drama that had been embedded in her head for all these years into a comedy. See how easy it can be to change your experience in certain situations?

So, when you're at your wit's end, hire Mel Brooks, and laugh it off!

7

ADVERTISING AND MEDIA

There are two ways to be fooled. One is to believe what isn't true; the other is to refuse to believe what is true.
—Kierkegaard

What other industry could get away with lying almost 100 percent of the time? The advertising industry misleads us and deceives us, and their claims are filled with inaccuracies. Media and politics are not much different. They all can sling shit your way and dress it up nicely wrapped.

Trickery, I Tell You!

One day, the jewelry industry got together for a meeting. This meeting was about how to make even more of a profit than they were already making. Someone came up with a brilliant idea—"How about we market the flawed and crappy diamonds as *champagne diamonds?*" The boss yelled out, "Brilliant, my boy! Let's run it up the flag post and see if anyone salutes it." It was a big hit.

As time passed, this bright young man had an even better idea. He suggested that the really shitty diamonds should be sold as *chocolate diamonds*. Again, big hit.

Fishermen who accidentally started catching a certain type of fish in their nets, rather than throw them back, sold them to restaurants, and they were served as the original name, which was *Patagonian toothfish*. This fish did not sell well. They renamed this fish *Chilean sea bass*. Same fish, but now a different name and a different result. It now became more popular.

The meat industry started to advertise that they now had corn-fed meat. They failed to mention that cows should not be eating corn. If a cow were to go from grass to corn right away, the cow would die. It takes six months for a cow to transition from eating grass to eating corn. This was a quick fad that faded out. The public got wise to the proper diet of a cow. Now, we are back to advertising that our cows are grass fed.

Mattresses were being advertised as a no-flip mattress. They should have called it *can't flip mattresses*. They were trying to sell you half the quality for the same price.

Years ago, I saw a commercial for a candy product. This commercial made a commitment to its viewers. They offered 70 percent more than before. I heard this kind of claim before from other candy companies of 20 or 30 percent, but never as much as 70 percent. This sounds like more of an apology than an advertisement. It's like the CEO is telling you, "Hey man, sorry but we've been screwing you for years, and this is our way of making it up to you. I hope there are no hard feelings. Oh, and by the way, we now put them in a box for you."

If you start to pay close attention to commercials, you may notice how deceptive they really are. These advertisements don't really tell you what to wear, drink, or drive, but they do a great job convincing you that you need what they have to offer. Many of these commercials will use envy as a strategy. They will put you through a rollercoaster of emotions. They make you feel sad, happy, guilty, healthy, or unhealthy. You name it. They could do it.

When it comes down to a prescription drug, you already know what you need because the commercial said so. The doctor is only the middle man here. It doesn't matter how long a doctor has been in practice; if he doesn't give you what you want, you will go seek it from another doctor.

Please Give Me a Hint

My agent sent me out on an audition for a product that you stick on your problem area for pain relief. The casting director and the director were holding this audition. The audition had no lines, all improv. They just wanted me to talk about how much this product helped me, so I did my spiel.

My agent called me the next day to inform me that I booked the job along with other actors. She also informed me that I must buy this product before we film on Monday. She insisted that I had to use it before the shoot. "Okay. Got it. No problem." And of course, they said they would reimburse me.

I went to the location, which was a house. They had the seven of us sit downstairs and wait for our names to be called to the set, which was on the main floor in the kitchen. Nobody was allowed to go upstairs until they were called. And no one was allowed to go back down after they were filmed. They had to exit the house and leave. We could not discuss the details of the filming, so we were all in the dark. And back then, cell phones were not common, so we couldn't relay any information to each other about it.

I was somewhat nervous because I had no lines to memorize, and I was unsure how I was going to react on the spot with questions thrown at me. I spotted a film crew guy I worked with months earlier in another commercial and secretly asked him what questions does the director ask the actors? He could not tell me, but he assured me it was very easy.

I heard my name called out and went upstairs. They quickly had me sit on a chair that was already mic'd, lighted, and ready to go. I felt like I was being interrogated by the FBI. This happened so fast and forceful that I was nervous. I never worked on a set quite like this before.

Before I could catch my breath, the director yelled, "Action!" He asked me while filming, "Would you say that product X helped you tremendously with your shoulder pain?" Wow, I thought. That was an easy question. So I replied with a great answer. "Yes, it did. My shoulder never felt better."

He yelled, "Cut!" and looked at me with great disappointment. What the fuck did I do wrong? He quickly yelled "Action!" again and repeated the same question as before: "Would you say that Product X helped you tremendously with your shoulder pain?" This time I answered the same way but with much more confidence than before. Then I thought to myself, "Me do good this time. Right, Boss?" He yelled "Cut!" once again. This time he looked angry, as though he wanted to break a two-by-four over my head. Again I thought, What the fuck, man? The crew member I mentioned earlier who I knew from another commercial got close to me and whispered to me to repeat *exactly* what the director was saying to me and say it right back to the camera the same way it left the director's mouth. Sweet Fancy Moses! Why didn't they just tell me that to begin with?

The director yelled, "Action!" and after he said, "Would you say …" I just repeated what he said: "Product X helped me tremendously with my shoulder pain." The next question the director asked me was, "Would you say Product X helped you with your pain more than any other product you've used before?" You see how easy acting can be? Sometimes you just have to be a parrot.

Oh, and the subtitles that you see on the bottom of your television screen that state "These are actual users" is true in this case because I was told to use it before we filmed. Do you see what I mean by the advertising industry? There is no deception whatsoever. It's all true.

I have a friend who worked in the advertising industry in New York City many years ago. The product they were advertising was a powdered cleaner that they claimed would be safe for all surfaces, including glass.

Her job was to start calling observatories throughout the country and asking if they could use this product on their telescope lenses, which were worth about a million dollars. They all said, "Absolutely not," until she called one observatory in the southwest who just replaced their telescope and would give them permission to use that product on their old lens. You see how this business is? Damn tyrants!

Goldfish

CNN once reported that a group of scientists studied goldfish. They determined that goldfish have a memory capacity of only three seconds.

For those of you who don't remember what was covered in the national news before the Trump administration, I will refresh your memory: various and countless stories and topics were covered. Not so much these days. Our White House has been reengineered to resemble a reality show.

So, when I heard about this goldfish story, I felt bad for this poor fish. But then I realized that this three-second memory capacity works in their favor. Goldfish have a pretty shitty life to begin with. I've never seen a goldfish in a nice, beautiful, big tank unless they were food for the big fish. They were always in a little bowl by themselves with that castle in the middle of the dirty water.

Since this fish has a three-second memory, he doesn't know he is in a small bowl. When he swims to the end of his bowl and hits the wall, he thinks he just ran into the end of the ocean because he doesn't remember hitting the other wall on the other side. And that castle in the middle is always new to him. He enters the castle and thinks, "Nice house. I wonder who lives here?" He probably doesn't know he is the only one in the tank. He may think he met someone earlier but just forgot. And that filthy water he swims in may just seem like a cloudy day to him. You see, this three-second rule is essential for his survival.

Imagine if this rule were applied to humans. It would be pure euphoria. You could borrow money and never have to give it back and never even have to feel guilty because neither party remembers. Your wife can cook shitty meatloaf, and by the time it goes from your mouth to your stomach, you forgot how bad it tasted. The only drawback would be watching movies. You will never have the slightest idea of who's who and what the hell is going on.

The best part of this for humans would be no more boredom with marriages. You go to sleep with one woman. The next morning you wake up thinking, "Well, well, well, who have we here?" You only need two positions when making love. But she'll think you're Valentino.

Get Your Stars Here! *****

To this day, I still don't understand how someone is permitted to sell stars. Once in a while, I hear a commercial on the radio that for fifty-two bucks you can have a star named after you. I'm not a business major, but if you're going to sell something, don't you have to own it first? How can one guy own all these stars? To my knowledge, Bill Gates and Warren Buffet don't even own stars. How can one guy corner this market?

However, if this guy is legit, fifty-two bucks is a very reasonable price for a star. A great deal if you ask me; however, I figured out how this guy keeps his prices so low. He is selling the same star to thousands of people. What a racket!

What are the chances that two people who bought the same star would ever meet? It's not like two women at a party would be sitting out on a dark, starry night on a balcony and one woman says to the other, "See that star? My boyfriend bought that star for me." And the other woman says, "Oh no, girl! You must be mistaken. My man got that star for me!" Yada, yada, yada—cat fight breaks out.

The news isn't so different from the advertising

industry. They have equal skill sets. Both can play with your emotions. Advertisers will run the same commercial over and over again until it sinks into your head.

One of my clients was a president for a major soft drink company. We were talking about advertising, and he told me that his company stopped advertising for one week while other soft drink companies continued to advertise. He informed me that in just that one week there was a big drop in sales, which to me confirms the statement, "Out of sight. Out of mind." It also proves to me just how programmed we can be.

Many years ago, the news reported a topic once and only once. I was very interested to hear more about this topic, but it disappeared. This topic came and went faster than a shooting star, never to be seen again.

It was reported that China found bugs (listening devices) on the seat cushions of airplanes that were made by America to be used by the Chinese government. I, myself found that this story was worthy of more exposure, but that would not be right, would it? Most Americans would be willing to turn a blind eye to this sort of information. After all, America, just like any other family, would not want to show their dirty laundry. I imagine a high government official put a stop to that bit of news that slipped through.

The news even has the same magical talent as David Copperfield, the famous magician. They can conceal, hide, suppress, and create distractions so the viewer remains clueless. Pure magic!

So what does it take for us as a people, a nation, a culture, a society, and a world to change for the better?

Must it take an event like 9/11 for politicians to act like grown, honorable men?

Will it take a magical carpet ride to space by all of us, especially world leaders, in order to truly see the world (earth) as one? Or do we continue to put all our efforts and resources to develop weapons of mass destruction? Do we continue to divide countries, only to continue to divide ourselves from each other? Must we continue to compete among each other in every aspect of our lives to the point where the winner and the loser is clearly determined?

What Is a Flag?

I never liked flags, even as a kid. I saw them as a symbol to separate, not to unite. The only place I want to see a flag is in a restaurant, so I know what kind of food I will be eating.

This topic may be arguable. I looked at it from many angles many times before, and I still think the same now as I did when I was younger. Some relatives of mine who lived in Brooklyn hung the Italian flag in front of their home. To me, I see it as, "Look at us. We're Italian, and you're not." Or "This is where an Italian family lives." I understand that people are proud of their heritage, but there are various ways to show it.

As a kid, I was able to walk into someone's home, and without seeing their faces or their last name, I could tell if they were Italian or Jewish just by looking at their couches. Couches covered in clear plastic were a dead giveaway that they were either Italian or Jewish. That's just what we did.

In winter, when we sat down, it would sound and feel like we were sitting on a couch made of taco shells. And in the hot, steamy summers, since my parents considered A/C a luxury and not a necessity, those same couches turned into an indoor slip and slide.

Another way you could tell if the family was Italian was by them man-powering food down your throat. If you were to walk into a home and were offered a drink, you would be in an Irish home.

I remember never sitting on my friends' couches in a non-Italian household. I always sat on the chairs or stood up for long periods of time. For me, sitting on a couch with no covers on it was a sign of disrespect. That's how sacred plastic covers were to Italians. Therefore, no flags were needed.

It's not just flags of countries but flags of states that I don't care for. No matter how you look at it, you are still separating yourself from your neighbors.

Even at sports events, people are fanatics about their logos and team uniforms. Many players get traded to different cities and states. Therefore, you are not rooting for the players themselves. As Jerry Seinfeld said, "You are basically rooting for the laundry."

But some people are so proud of where they came from and are adamant to show it. But I say, "Who cares?" It's not where we're from; it's where we are now.

My state is better than yours. My team is better than yours. My country is better than yours. And most of all, my religion is better than yours. It would be nice if every nation on this earth would agree on one flag. It has to be cool looking and very hip, and together, we can kick any planet's ass!

What kind of world is this where we create and celebrate the power we have over each other? Instead, we ought to celebrate the mere existence of this perfect world we are blessed to live in.

Is this what life is about? If so, I want to get off at the next stop on this crazy train! It can be done. I've seen it done by many people. They change their whole attitude about life. The problem is that only one person exits the train at a time. Usually the brave and wise ones catch on.

What Are You Waiting For—Smoke?

I saw a study on television years back on human behavior. People were put together in groups in a classroom setting to fill out surveys, which they would get paid to do. Cameras were placed in different locations throughout the classroom. The facilitator would leave the classroom once the instructions were given. There was a smoke-making machine concealed behind the front door of the classroom, and after about fifteen minutes into their surveys, the participants would notice smoke coming from under the door. This study was conducted to see how long it would take the participants to exit the classroom and get to safety.

The reaction of people noticing the smoke was very clear because of all the cameras throughout the room. The interesting things about each classroom video was that even though people observed the smoke coming from under the door, they did not take any action. They simply looked to others in the room to see if anyone else noticed the possible danger. And there were others who did. However, the group did not take action, even though they knew they were in danger, until the first person in the room actually stood up from his seat to exit the door to seek safety. Then everyone else followed.

So what this study shows me is that even though people are not comfortable or even safe with what is going on in their lives, they will wait until that *one person* takes action before they do.

Going back to the people who exit this crazy train, they don't need to see the smoke before they exit because they smell it first. They are the brave and courageous ones who take the first step when they see themselves in a bad scene. They know they don't need to conform to the others around them and what society has bestowed upon them.

So there you have it, folks! The greatest show on earth.
Don't forget to tip your servers and bartenders.
We'll be here all week … and the week after … and after.
Sincerely,
Rule-makers of the World

8

BE COMFORTABLE WITH BEING UNCOMFORTABLE

*Do the thing you fear and the death
of fear is certain.*
—Ralph Waldo Emerson

I am truly glad we live in a free country. We have endless possibilities and opportunities; however, I believe many people are still confined to social shackles. Many of us are imprisoned by criticism and not conforming to the norm.

How do we get comfortable with just being ourselves? How far can we get in life if we remain overly concerned about what others think of us and our actions? As long as we are not hurting anyone emotionally or physically, what does it matter what others think? After all, this is your life, not theirs. Some people will criticize you no matter what you do, so just expect it and live with it.

Many of my clients admitted that they chose their careers or positions at a workplace because they wanted to be free of criticism. They very much would have liked different jobs or positions, but it would have entailed public speaking and having to be responsible for others.

Let's examine two completely different careers in the same exact industry. One is a filmmaker and the other is a film critic. The person who makes films puts no limit on him- or herself. He/She knows that taking chances is part of his/her success. He/She doesn't put very much weight on what others think of him/her. He/She just wants to show and express him- or herself.

Now, take a film critic. This person prefers to criticize

rather than to be criticized. His/Her job is to inform the public what is right and what is wrong with a particular movie.

One of these careers is a player and the other a spectator. The director would clearly be more comfortable with being uncomfortable. He/She is a player.

So how does someone begin and master the skill of being comfortable with being uncomfortable? The good news is that it is much easier than you think and can be mastered very quickly, and most of all, it is fun.

Let me make something clear to you. This game, for lack of a better word, is fun. However, you will get bored unless you continually raise your bar, which is good news. You will begin to get comfortable with the little things that were at first making you feel uncomfortable, which translates into perhaps boredom for some people. So you keep raising the bar higher and higher. Then you will come to realize that all the fears you had about taking action were not fears at all. They were opportunities, possibilities, potential, and buried talent.

The way I started being comfortable with being uncomfortable was by taking baby steps. I began with various, random things that mattered to me. I will briefly mention a baby step and later go into detail with big-boy steps.

I always thought that the fact that most people didn't make eye contact in an elevator shared by two or three people was downright rude. Here we are stepping into a form of transportation with a stranger for only a few seconds. There are no windows to look out like a taxi or a bus, and no time to read because of the time limits. Just four boring walls in a tiny square compartment. So for anyone to stare at the floor of this box as if they were staring at a glass-bottom boat over a coral reef in the Virgin Islands is rude and uncivil. So I decided to put a stop to this, one elevator at a time. I began giving a simple "hi" with brief eye contact when I entered an elevator or when someone else entered one. Like I said, it was a small and simple step, but something that I personally wanted to work on, which led to bigger and better things. Now, if I said good-bye to someone as they exited or I exited, that would be sufficient cause for a restraining order. That would just be weird. So I hope you have an idea of what I mean when I say small things.

Jet-Setter

In the early '80's, I worked for an airline. My friends and I took full advantage of the flight benefits, and I considered myself a jet-setter. I took trips from coast to coast and overseas with only one night's notice. So I went again and again with my airline buddies, traveling like Frank Sinatra and the Rat Pack. I was comfortable traveling because I was always with my friends. We were always around each other, no matter where we were.

One day just before a trip to Los Angeles, my two friends canceled on me last minute. I was pissed off and also had some anxiety about doing this alone. But I went on my own in spite. I remembered thinking as the plane took off, "Why the hell am I going? What the hell will I do on my own? I will be walking the streets of LA day and night with no one and no particular place to go, like the walking dead. I should have stayed home."

What an eye-opening experience it was for me. I was surprised how comfortable I became with each encounter with a total stranger. I noticed that I was more outgoing and social when I was not with my traveling buddies because I had no choice but to be. I felt liberated, unattached, and uninhibited—all because I had no goals. I never planned my day, and I was able to change my mind at any given time without checking with anyone. Looking back now, I know I had a great time because I had no goals. I did have an *intention*, though, which was to just enjoy where I was and just be. I was so excited by this revelation that I never traveled again with my airline buddies. I decided that every trip from that moment on was going to be a solo mission. This really opened my life up in many ways. I know I can travel and be on my own and be comfortable in many situations that once would have scared me. So what I first feared about traveling was something that I began to embrace. All these wonderful experiences I had traveling originated in my mind as fear.

Asking a Stranger to Lunch

There was a point in my life where my massage career was no longer cutting it. So I decided to try getting into the advertising business since I was creative. I knew nothing of the advertising field, and information back then was not so easy to find, unlike today. Google was not around. And I wasn't willing to take college courses just to find out more about it. I did not know anyone who was in this field either.

Be Comfortable with Being Uncomfortable

So I picked up a public business phonebook and started calling advertising companies in my city and asked the receptionist if someone in the office would be willing to have lunch "on me" in exchange for information on a career in the advertising industry.

The first few companies I called were not open to my request, and they may have thought I was strange, but honestly by this age, I didn't care what a stranger thought. So I continued calling until I found a receptionist who was receptive to my request and would pass the word along. I immediately got a call back from a guy who I assumed was the hungriest in the office. He was very nice and assured me that by the time our lunch meeting was over, I would know if this field was right for me or not. I surely did. It turns out, "me no like!" I could not see myself being creative with the stress of the deadlines.

So, in order for me to get this kind of information straight from the horse's mouth, I had to get past my comfort zone about making the initial phone call. I realized that I would have no problem doing something like this again. I was becoming more and more comfortable with each uncomfortable situation that came up.

Why Acting?

I've mentioned throughout this book that I dabbled in acting. Just to clarify this topic, I stopped acting just prior to reaching my pinnacle. I did so to deny this cold-hearted, unfair, filthy, vial, and unethical industry of my wonderful and brilliant abilities. I did this out of malice, and to this day I am proud of it. Not very many people knew about my absence from this industry. Now that I think back, the only ones who knew about my departure from the industry were my agent and me.

So, when I started pursuing acting, I had no experience, no training, and no talent. I only had a headshot and unbridled enthusiasm. I was simply hoping for the element of surprise.

After pounding the streets of New York City, merely lacking experience, training, and talent, I clearly saw the result of my labor. I decided to get help from an organization that didn't really teach you how to act but drew from you why you want to act in the first place. It consisted of actors supporting each other and learning from each other. Each week, we broke down into different groups and expressed our experiences in the industry. Almost all of them were working actors who were on soaps, commercials, and films. I was the only one at the time that had never worked as an actor. At the end of the course, we each had chosen a monologue and went on stage to be critiqued by our peers. I chose a David Mamet monologue because I took pleasure in cursing, and it came to me naturally.

I went on stage and took a few moments to breathe. I looked into the crowd, and out of my mouth came nothing of David Mamet's works. Instead, words came out that I never rehearsed before. It was as if I was temporarily possessed and someone was talking through me. I can't remember exactly what I said or in what order I said it. I only remember muttering that I wanted to teach people to be happy in this life, not to take life too seriously, and that happiness can be found almost anywhere if you look for it. This muttering went on for two more minutes.

After I was done, they continued to stare at me as though I had more to say, but I didn't. They all clapped and seemed entertained about what I just said, and I didn't understand why. The females in the crowd stood up to give their opinion on my performance. I found out that they liked to see vulnerability in men. I was told that to be a good actor you have to show yourself and your weaknesses. I guess I did a good job at that because they loved to see that in me.

That was thirty years ago. It makes sense to me now. I was trying to teach people what I needed to learn, and I think I'm doing pretty good. And I will continue to learn.

Stand-Up

While working on a set for a commercial, I met an actor who was very funny and made everyone laugh to the point of peeing our pants. At the end of the shoot, I made him aware of how funny I thought he was. "I hope so. I am a comedian for a living." His response was no surprise to me. He informed me that he taught comedy.

"How do you teach comedy? How can you teach someone to be funny?" I replied.

"I don't teach anyone to be funny. They are already funny. They just don't know it yet." He also let me know that his students had to perform on stage at a comedy club after his last class. I quickly signed up for his class.

I'm the kind of person who likes to try new things. I did not focus on the fact that I had to be on stage for ten minutes at a comedy club, something that most people would fear. Instead, I focused on all that I would learn in that six weeks and how much I could use that experience in my life.

The classes were held in an old business complex. The room was what you would see in an average high school. We all sat on wooden chairs and desks. Our comedy teacher also had a large desk in front of the classroom. Not a place to teach comedy, I thought to myself.

Our class was very diverse. They ranged from actors to school teachers, and there was a woman who was a meteorologist for CNN, who was very comfortable in front of the camera.

On the first day, our teacher went over the basics. He asked what type of comedian we'd like to be: ranging from Jerry Seinfeld, one who is observational to Carrot Top, who uses props. He also gave us homework, which was to keep a pen and pad with us all week to write down anything we observed that was funny.

At first, I thought this homework would be very difficult. It was far from it. When I looked for funny things in life, I spotted it right away. Just like life itself. You will find whatever you focus on—good or bad. It all depends on which glasses you choose to wear.

All the material I needed for the comedy class came to me in a matter of just a few hours. It was easy. The next time we met in class, we had to do our thing. There were at least fifteen people in that class, but only a few who were funny, in my opinion.

There was a guy in the class, who at that time I thought had no business being there. He looked like a disgruntled, retired postal worker taking comedy classes just to spark up his apparently dull life. It was evident to me, and perhaps to

Be Comfortable with Being Uncomfortable

others, that this guy did not own a comb or a mirror. From the way he dressed, it didn't seem as though he had a light in his closet.

He told stories about what he saw on local news regarding child pornography and pedophiles, neither of which were pleasant to hear, especially from a comical point of view. I did not care for the material he chose and how he said it. I, along with other students, felt bad for him. How could he go on stage with this act?

At the end of that night, the teacher critiqued our work and gave each of us advice, not on the material we chose but *how* to say it. The guy with the pedophile story was told to use the same material and say it the same way he did before. The only thing the teacher told him to change was to try not to make anyone laugh with this topic. He said to make it very serious and that he, this particular student, is the victim of what he was hearing on the news. How the hell is that going to make this guy funny? Maybe this teacher isn't so good after all, I thought to myself. The following week this student did his act in front of the class. After a minute into his act, no one in the class could hear what he was saying because half of the students were off their seats and laughing their asses off, including the teacher and myself. I hadn't laughed that much in years.

This student started his act by letting everyone know that he didn't appreciate the news pandering to him. He was playing the victim. And he showed everyone how upset and infuriated it made him. This person's topic had no humor, nor should it have been a subject to joke about. He did a great job convincing us that he was truly the victim. I gave him credit for being comfortable with this unpleasant material he chose to use. I gave him even more credit that he decided to stick with the same material after he witnessed how harsh a response he received from the class his first time up. I, myself, would have refused to use that topic again if I had been rejected like that.

The comedy club we performed in was an actual club called Funny Farm in Atlanta. Before the club opened, our teacher had us go on stage to practice our ten-minute set. When it was my turn to practice, I looked at the empty seats and started my routine. I was lost for words. I knew what I had to say, but somehow I couldn't piece my act together. My teacher looked at me and said, "What the hell, John? You're going to be on in an hour." I was calm, and I confidently let him know that I couldn't do this if no one was out there in the seats. I told him I would be fine once the seats were full.

I never liked to rehearse for anything! For me, I never gave 100 percent for rehearsals. I treated rehearsals as a false fire drill. Yeah, I would follow the proper steps and exit the burning building that was not really on fire, but there was no emotion or energy behind it. But if this building was on fire, believe me; I would have been *on!*

Once the club opened and I was introduced by my teacher, I did fine. The first minute was a little frightening, but once I got my first laugh, it was like a miracle drug that suddenly kicked in, and my mind and body relaxed.

As for the material I used for open mic, you have been reading it throughout this book. Some of the things I used were the stories about the goldfish, stars, and candy, in addition to some other stories not in this book.

I never enjoyed working as an actor as much as I did

doing stand-up, and I didn't get paid a cent. I didn't have to get into a certain character or hide behind one. It was all me—my own thoughts and lines, and I did it my way. Best feeling ever!

Stalag 17

When I first started pursuing acting, I auditioned for a play for the part of Lieutenant Dunbar in *Stalag 17*, a play about a German POW camp. At this early stage of my life, I sucked as an actor, but I didn't care. Or maybe I didn't even know I was so bad. But I auditioned for it anyway. Back then, I had no problem with rejection from a stranger, and I would brush it off my shoulder as if it was dandruff.

After my poor audition, I walked out to my car to drive home. The director came out to the parking lot and approached me right before I drove away. He offered me a part in the play and thought I would be perfect for it. He explained that I would not have a speaking role, but I would be on stage the entire play, more than any other actor. I had never heard of such a thing. I wasn't sure if I was just offered a part in the play as a potted plant.

The character he offered me was a soldier named Horney, who was shell-shocked and could no longer speak. I agreed to it. Boy, did I have fun playing this character! I could do no wrong. Every night I did something different than the night before. No one could critique my performance. Not only did I not have any lines to learn, I didn't even have to learn the blocking. I could do whatever I wanted, when and how I wanted to.

One night before our show, the director informed us

that there would be a critic from the *New York Times* in the audience. Everyone was nervous, but not me. It was a great feeling to do what I wanted and not get judged. When the *New York Times* review came out, it gave two very favorable reviews on two of the seventeen actors. I was one of them. How can anyone not be comfortable playing that part? I felt no pressure to impress, only to be in the moment of the scene.

Stir-Crazy

I think it would do us all good to serve one month in solitary confinement. Along with food and water, we also would need pen and paper. I believe this could change our lives. It could leave us with no other option but to reflect. Reflecting is something that is needed by all of us and something that should be done periodically. We get lost in the bullshit around us, and we start believing in our own bullshit if we don't take time to reflect. For me, reflecting is asking myself important questions such as, Am I doing what I really want to do with my life? Am I following my own inner guidance, or am I being influenced by outside sources? Asking powerful questions like these can really help a person grow.

I was massaging a woman at a resort for the second time. She had come to see me a year prior. She informed me that at the time of her last visit with me she was very stressed out. Her son was in jail in Central America for not having proper papers to visit that country. She also told me that her son's time spent in jail was one of the best experiences he had ever had and changed his life.

Be Comfortable with Being Uncomfortable

While the other people in jail were going crazy and losing their minds, he kept calm. He took the opportunity to reflect on his life and think about what changes he needed to make. What kind of discoveries came out of this I could not tell you, nor do I know. All I know is that this woman told me that he was grateful for this occurrence and he was working on a book about his experience.

In the movie *Stir Crazy*, with Gene Wilder and Richard Pryor, Gene Wilder was kept in solitary confinement. When it was time for the warden to let him out of his small, dark cell, Gene Wilder's character pleaded with the warden that he needed more time in confinement because he was just getting to know himself.

I believe this character started to know himself because he had no outside information to distract him, like TV, news, media, or even other people. Nothing was programming his mind. Therefore, he had to think on his own without outside influences.

I can tell you from my own personal experience regarding my goals or intentions, and perhaps you may see it for yourself in your own experience, that I get much more accomplished physically and mentally when I don't fill my time with these distractions. Basically, any rubbish I can avoid, I will. I don't want you to think I'm a lunatic. I did watch *Seinfeld* and *Breaking Bad*—let's get real!

Social media can be evil if not used properly, especially for kids and teenagers. Many teenagers only know who they are by social media and by what other peeps think of them. Growing up, I never had that problem. Social media was only the handful of friends I had. We never compared ourselves to anybody.

A good quote about reflection is one by Carl Jung: "Who looks outside, dreams; who looks inside, awakes."

Fear of Relocating

For many people, fear of relocating is a difficult transition. Many factors are involved, like putting a house on the market, leaving good friends, having to meet new people, starting a new job, and other annoyances. With that attitude about leaving your hometown, why would anyone have a desire to leave unless they were put in the witness protection program?

I have moved many times and do not find it difficult at all. I look at it as an opportunity, not as a risk. I look at it as a gain and not a loss. Don't think I treat people like objects. I still keep in touch with the friends I knew when I move. Another quote by Carl Jung that fits here nicely is, "Don't hold onto someone who's leaving; otherwise, you won't meet the one who's coming." This quote is not only true with people but can be applied in many other ways. If you want a new career, you cannot hold onto your old career. I welcome new experiences and new surroundings. Some people are fine just staying where they are, and that's cool too. But I'm talking about those who truly want to move to a new location.

The first time I relocated, I was very uncomfortable. I was stressed and had many sleepless nights. Not so much now. I've gotten more comfortable each time I've moved. I do have to say I enjoy where I am now, but I am open to change if needed.

To Pill, or Not to Pill? That Is the Question.

I took pills to make me feel comfortable. I drank to make me feel comfortable. And I ate more than my body required for survival. It was a quick fix. It never solved my issues. It just made them manageable for a moment, and only a moment.

I did this because I knew no other way to deal with my issues. And learning how to would mean I had to work hard at figuring it all out. And if I did learn how, that would mean that every time a problem arose, I would have had to do a lot of freakin' homework, which I tried to avoid. So why wouldn't I just continue taking pills, drinking, and eating as if I was preparing for hibernation? It's because life sucked that way. I wasn't learning or growing by doing those numbing activities. I was simply managing my issues rather than addressing them.

My life was stagnant, like Bill Murray's life in the movie *Groundhog Day*. I was just waiting for my life to be over. I had no intention of hurting myself, but I did wish the clock would move much faster, so I could finally rest in peace. This was my attitude for a period of time in my life, but I still had the other half of my life left to live.

I stopped taking pills for anxiety and depression. I am not telling the reader to stop medication. Medication is of great benefit for many people and could improve their lives. I am simply sharing my own experience with medication. The reason I chose to go on medication in the first place was because I was not aware of what was causing my depression and anxiety. Even if I had known what caused it, I wouldn't have known how to begin helping myself through it.

At this point, I know what causes it, and I know how to correct it. This does not mean I don't get depressed. I still do, but only for a fraction of the time I did before. I don't wait until I get depressed to try to figure out why I got depressed. I catch it at its early stage, which is sadness. I don't hide it under the rug. I acknowledge it, accept it, and play *detective* to try to figure it out. The more I play detective, the better and faster I get at solving it.

I don't mind feeling blue once in a while. I actually embrace it. This is a sign that my path in life needs to be adjusted. That being said, I strongly agree with someone who has been bombarded unexpectedly with such high levels of stress to consider medication to help get through that period. It may be too much for anyone to handle.

I don't drink anymore. I don't drink any less either. I just don't drink any more than I had before. All kidding aside, I was still drinking after I stopped taking medication. I was so proud that I was off medication that I justified it with drinking. I thought I was in control of my drinking. I'm not sure what constitutes a drinking problem. I would never drink and drive, and I would never show up somewhere buzzed. I do enjoy a glass of wine or beer at lunch on my days off, and I would have a drink or two at night. Some days it would add up to three drinks a day. I guess that is a lot. But I controlled it! This is when I started to believe my own bullshit; however, it always controlled me. I noticed that I wasn't very productive when I drank too much, and it only made me sad if I had too much in one day. I came up with a brilliant idea. What if I didn't buy any wine or beer? This way if I craved a

Be Comfortable with Being Uncomfortable

drink, it would be nowhere to be found. This worked better than I thought. Genius! I could go a week or two without a drink. Maybe I didn't have a drinking problem, but I sometimes consumed more than I needed to.

I took medication and alcohol to feel comfortable when I felt uncomfortable. I thought there was nothing else for me to take control of that would help me have a healthier life and a clearer and sharper mind, so I could be the best I could be in this life of mine. I was wrong again. A wise man told me that if I eat right, exercise, and get enough sleep, it would make me feel and perform better. I knew what he told me must be true. I am sure of it because I'd heard that same statement used before by idiots, dimwits, and doofuses. I will not lecture you on this topic, but I started this absurd way of living, and it is changing my mind, body, and spirit. Holy shit! They were right.

In life, if you continue to cover a wound that needs proper attention with merely a Band-Aid, it is equivalent to using an infected Band-Aid. It will only get worse with time.

So that is how I began to get comfortable with situations that I personally needed to overcome. My elevator story did not begin with the sole purpose of only making eye contact in elevators. I knew if I got comfortable making eye contact in a confined area, that would lead me to connecting with people everywhere else, from the streets to social events. Once I mastered that, the fear went away.

I then raised the bar to other areas that needed to be worked on in order to improve myself. The fear that started with every endeavor pretty much dissipated. Not only did the fear diminish but also the byproduct of fear—anxiety, worry, stress, and despair.

I think it is impossible to be fearless. But you must put fear on the back burner and focus on what you want to cook at that time. Not focusing on your fear will lead to change, which will then lead to growth.

9

BELIEVE IT UNTIL YOU BECOME IT!

> *Optimism is the faith that leads to achievement. Nothing can be done without hope and confidence.*
> —Helen Keller

We've all heard the phrase, "Fake it until you make it." It is a good phrase, but it needs to be improved if you want it to work for you. So I want you to delete "fake it until you make it" from your memory bank in your head and replace it with "believe it until you become it."

Just the word *fake* makes my stomach turn. There is nothing positive about that word. That word travels with other negative words such as *phony, false, bogus, imitation, fraud, hoax,* and *liar.* All these words are vile. This new phrase is a positive one and will work in your favor.

Years ago, I saw these magnetic bracelets on commercials claiming that simply wearing them would give you more power. They showed how people's muscle strength improved when wearing these bracelets as opposed to when they were not wearing them.

I will prove to you that these bracelets really do work. And at the same time, I can prove to you that these bracelets don't work at all. I am 100 percent sure of these two very different outcomes. What am I talking about? Well, step right up folks, and gather around, and I will tell you a secret about how these bracelets work and about how you can make anything work in your life.

It's not the bracelet that gives you the strength. It is the *belief* that you give to the bracelet that gives you the strength.

If you don't believe in the bracelet's powers, it simply will not do anything for you except for the aesthetics.

Imagine the unlimited potential you can give yourself if you applied this kind of belief in your life? If you don't have any belief in whatever you attempt to do in life, you are merely showing up as a spectator. This falls into what Woody Allen has said: "Showing up is 80 percent of life."

Grip

A grip is a part of the technician crew in film and video production. At a time when I thought of becoming a grip for a living, I decided to learn more about it on an actual movie set. It made sense to me. So I snuck into the filming of a Woody Allen movie in New York City.

This building had security on every entrance and exit. This was a time when no one wore identification badges. I decided to walk in like I belonged there. I opened the first door of the building where security was stationed. However, I opened that first door as if I knew what was behind that door, when in reality I did not know. I said hi to security and walked right past them and opened another door that I thought led somewhere, but it did not. It was an equipment room. I could not simply close that door and walk away empty-handed, otherwise they would know that I did not belong. I grabbed some small wooden platforms and walked out with them. I didn't actually know what they were used for, but I took them anyway. I decided to head toward the double doors away from security for two reasons: I wanted to distance myself from security and also to get behind those double doors because I thought they would lead to something much more than just a broom closet. Behind this door was the stage itself. It was dark, and I heard the voices of the actors coming from the middle of this large room. I slowly walked closer to the filming and blended myself with the crew.

It took about an hour before I was approached by Woody Allen's key grip. He politely asked who I was, and I answered honestly, saying I wanted to know more about being a grip. He allowed me to stay and observe him working with his crew. He was very nice.

The reason I got into that building and through security was because they believed I belonged there, only because *I* took on the belief that I belonged there. So security didn't question it.

To take this story even further, I hatched another brilliant scheme. I was such a big fan of Woody Allen that I wanted my headshot given to him directly from his key grip rather than his casting directors, which I had sent before with no luck.

I walked into the office of Local 52, the grip union in New York City. I asked where I could find the key grip. I mentioned his name. The person at the desk asked why, but he didn't say it in a nice way. It was more like a "What the hell do you want?" way. I told him that I had photos of possible film locations that this key grip wanted to look at. I showed him the manila envelope that I was holding; however, inside contained my headshot and résumé and a letter pleading to this key grip to personally give this to Woody Allen himself. Back then, today's technology was not around, so that envelope containing the photos had no other way of getting to him.

The man behind the desk informed me that the key grip was out of the office for two weeks. "I was told he needed these ASAP," I said. Because I said it with such confidence and ease, the man wrote down the key grip's home address on a piece of paper and handed it to me with no thought at all, like he was handing me a piece of candy.

I mailed the envelope to the address written on the paper. I never received a call from Woody Allen. I don't even think this key grip ever gave my information to him. Maybe he thought I was not wrapped too tight. Oh well.

Reiki? Sure!

I worked for a resort that offered a treatment that included massage, shiatsu, and reiki combined. The therapist who performed this service called out sick, and it was a 9:00 a.m. appointment, which left no time for a replacement. The spa director asked if I could give this treatment to a woman client who was very much looking forward to it. My spa director knew that I was certified in shiatsu but not reiki and asked if I could fake my way through this treatment. I reluctantly agreed.

The woman let me know that she'd had this service before, which made me a little more nervous. I knew very little about reiki, and I was a recipient years ago, but I fell asleep during the last forty-five minutes of that fifty-minute treatment.

I gave her the treatment, thinking I was doing okay. She walked out of the room at the end of the treatment and let me know that that was the best reiki she had ever experienced.

Believe It until You Become It!

In this case, I was forced to muster up the confidence and belief in myself in order to pull off this service.

A month later, I took a class in reiki to find out more about it. I learned that I had already been giving this form of treatment in my regular massages with my clients. Go figure!

Fancy-Schmancy

I worked in an upscale resort as a banquet waiter. A group had arranged to have a dinner in which the chef himself personally explained the preparation of the dinner and answered any questions from the guests. A big problem arose at another banquet function that needed the chef's immediate attention. Therefore, the chef could not attend his original function with these guests.

A French banquet server who worked with me had a very strong accent, which made it very difficult to understand him. Management appointed him chef for the night for that particular group, who had paid extra for the other chef. Management briefly filled him in on the menu and let the ship sail. This French waiter completed the task at hand and did it so well that only one person had a question. He exaggerated his accent to the point where no one could understand what he was saying. No one dared ask him any more questions after the first poor soul asked if the meat was marinated. The chef (fake chef) made him feel like a buffoon after the first question was asked. Just like the soup Nazi. This coworker of mine was very unique. I never met anyone quite like him. He spoke French and Spanish perfectly but only understood English.

Confidence sells. It sells even better if you believe what you are selling. You can apply this to many areas in your life and to many occupations. There are some jobs in which you cannot simply fake it. As a layman, you can't expect to walk into an operating room and take over the surgery.

In chapter six, I mentioned that I didn't believe I was an actor until I got paid as one. I first showed up at my auditions as someone who wanted to be an actor rather than an actor showing up to play a part. A big difference, if you ask me. I would have gotten a lot more gigs if I had been aware of this. "I could have been somebody. I could have been a contender." My agent should have looked out for me. So what do I get? A one-way ticket to Palookaville.

Maybe I Do Have a Chance

After I moved out of New York, I gave up acting. Why bother? I barely got any work there. So why should I expect to get work elsewhere?

Before I moved, I worked as a waiter in a restaurant in New York City with someone who was an actor. This guy had the looks, the voice, and the talent. At the time we worked together, he was trying to get work and would invite agents to his shows. I was hit by reality. "What are the chances I could get decent work when a guy with everything going for him is struggling?"

Just over ten years later and two states behind me, I've seen my friend in many commercials. Then I saw him starring in his own TV show on a major network. That is when I justified myself on getting back into the business. He made it big. Maybe perhaps now I have a chance, I thought.

Believe It until You Become It!

I did take that chance, and it worked out better than I expected. I booked a lot of work and even booked a few national commercials. I made really good money.

Looking back on my life, I realized how much I accomplished during the periods in which I was optimistic. Along with my optimism, I always envisioned myself doing a particular activity that I wanted to manifest. I also made myself have the experience of that activity. And before I knew it, I was actually doing what I imagined.

Another very important reason I took on these endeavors with minimal fear was because I truly believed I was playing with house money. I had nothing to lose and a lot to gain. Rejection was something I was willing to put up with in order for me to gain the reward. If I were to look like an idiot with each attempt, that would mean that one more stranger in this world would think I'm an idiot. Big deal!

10

HEROES—WHO NEEDS THEM?

Don't forget, you are the hero of your own life story.
—Greg Boyle

If you ever get a chance to meet your hero, chances are you may be disappointed. My intention in this chapter is not to put down any celebrity of any kind. My intention is to inspire you to look up to yourself and see the potential you have and never feel like you are not enough. People only feel less than others when they compare themselves to others.

I'd like to share some short stories with you about celebrities, not to put them down but so we can see them in a different light.

Do as I Say, Not as I Do

A famous doctor gave a weeklong seminar at a resort where I worked. People came from all over the country and paid very good money to see and learn from him.

I gave him a massage and asked my usual questions prior to beginning the massage. Questions such as, Are there any areas of concern? What type of pressure? It was winter, and I asked if he would like the electric blanket turned on to keep him warm. He said yes.

The next evening, I massaged a woman who was so excited to be at the resort. She told me how much she was learning from his seminar. "That's great," I replied. I asked her the same questions I had asked the doctor, including if she would like the electric blanket on to keep her warm. "Oh no. Dr. XYZ said never to lay on an electric blanket. It's not good for you." So I left the blanket off.

This woman followed and trusted whatever this doctor said. And this doctor had the balls to pull a shenanigan like this to people who worship him. It wouldn't surprise me if his diet included Twinkies. I couldn't tell that woman the truth. I would have gotten fired for sure.

Welcome Back

At another resort where I worked, a certain male celebrity frequently visited. After numerous complaints from the male massage therapists to management about sexual advances made by this celebrity, he was finally banned from staying there. This kind of information wasn't made public until after more than ten years. What took so long, I don't know.

As an employee of these high-end resorts, the employees are to keep privacy in mind. My question is, *To what extent?* If any guest is sexually harassing an employee, as a victim a person should be able to press charges, or at least not conceal their actions. But the resorts don't because of the power these celebrities have, bringing money and prestige to the resort. Most hotels would fire you if you pursued an issue like that.

A female massage therapist in Scotland got fired because she pursued action against a male celebrity who was being inappropriate during his treatment.

Heroes—Who Needs Them?

Perhaps now, with all these recent cases coming out and the MeToo movement, change may occur.

I think all these celebrities who have enough money to pay off these settlements should simply run a tab on escort services instead. It all stays private. So it's not just about the sex. It's about the power. It's a major factor as to why they do it.

Fore, and Many, Many More

A young woman who I worked with entered the break room and told everyone she fucked a famous golfer the previous night. None of us doubted her for a second. I always assumed, just like everyone else, that he was an All-American who was looked up to. We all thought he had a perfect life with a beautiful wife and kids.

Two years later, his excessive infidelity was made public. No surprise to us who knew of his behavior years earlier.

Some of these celebrities don't actually commit a crime, unless one would consider it a moral crime. Believe me, I know women who would do anything for a chance to sleep with these celebrities. So the only real victims are the families.

He Doesn't Feel So Good

While working security in a New York City hotel, I received a call that a woman was screaming hysterically from the penthouse. I responded to the call. When I knocked on the door, there was no answer, but I still heard loud screaming. I used my key to enter the suite. This hysterical woman brought me to the bedroom to show me the dead body of a music icon. I couldn't believe who and what I saw. He was spread out cold, not moving an inch, even with her screaming and poking at him. I picked up the phone on the night table to call 911, when he slowly forced two words out of his mouth, which were "Don't call." It was a relief that he wasn't dead. So instead, I told him I would call the hotel doctor. The doctor came and confirmed that he overdosed, but it was not fatal.

The next day the New York City papers read that he canceled his concert because of the flu. The funny thing about this was four years later and twelve hundred miles away, he performed for a group in the resort where I worked as a waiter. I worked his table. While taking his order, I didn't think it would be cool to let him know I was the guy in the hotel room the night he overdosed.

Spa Délirant

Délirant is French for "delusional." I once worked in such a place. This resort prides itself as being a Zen place to visit to learn how to live a more peaceful, grounded life with less stress.

The funny thing about this particular resort is that the owners, managers, and teachers could have benefitted from attending the classes they offered ... because they surely didn't live it.

This environment was nothing like what they preached. This was a truly toxic environment. Management actually told us, their employees, "This resort does not care about you, your feelings, or your concerns about work conditions. The therapists who are immoral can do whatever they want as long as they make money for the resort." The managers had sex with waitresses and therapists. And the company turned a blind eye to this kind of behavior.

Most companies are all about the bottom line. This resort was no exception. Actually, this resort would make a great reality show.

So, as you can see, it's not just heroes we put our trust in but organizations such as this one. For those of you who want to improve and enrich your lives, visit Spa Délirant. When I first started working there, it was a place where it was all about the healing. Now, with corporations buying these resorts, it is a place where it's all about the business. But wait; there's more. They have plans to open more of these resorts throughout the country.

The Life of a Celebrity

Let's examine the life of a celebrity. Most of them start young, and at this young age they have no choice but to see themselves as a commodity. Within time, their reality compass is a little off. With more time, it works very poorly. And they often turn to alcohol and drugs and end up in rehab.

I didn't start auditioning until I was in my early twenties. It was not a good experience. I felt like the industry didn't give a shit about me as a person. I was okay with that because after all, it's a business, and I get that. But for kids, it must be rough.

Auditions are not like a job interview, where they want

to know about you, your hobbies, and your interests. As an actor, you enter the building, you are given lines to look over, then you are called in, take your mark, slate your name, and go. I would think for kids they could at least give them ice cream cones with sprinkles to make them cozy.

So, when these kids or young people come to an audition, they basically have to entertain the casting people. So the approval of the casting director is taken in as a form of conditional love, which may lead to distortion of relationships in their future.

As these actors get more famous, we assist them with their distortion. People kiss their asses 24-7, and they accept it and soon come to expect it.

I would not be wrong to say that a good portion of actors are not happy because of the jealousy and rejection and highs and lows of the business. Female actors are usually more sensitive than male actors, who look at it more like a business.

Let's Keep Things in Order

I was setting up my massage table for an in-room massage for an actress who to this day has a popular TV series. I was setting up across from her bedroom. Her bedroom door was wide open, and she was lying down in the middle of her bed with two other women sitting on each side of her bed, listening to her vent. I couldn't help but look and listen to the conversation myself as I was getting the table ready.

I noticed how sad she was. It was as though someone she cared about had died or was about to die. She was not

Heroes—Who Needs Them?

in tears, but close to it. I witnessed the other two women being compassionate to her feelings.

She was in no hurry to get on the table, even though her scheduled appointment was twenty minutes ago. So I had nothing to do but wait and listen even further.

My guess was correct. Someone was dying. It was her ego.

One of her female costars was getting more and more airtime as the series went on. She expressed to the other two women how unfair this was. This actress failed to see her industry for what it truly was. It was not about the loyalty or friendship. It was all about the money.

I myself recently started to realize that any business is about money, not just Hollywood. I truly can't think of any business where money is not the bottom line. Hospitals, where people go for help and care, is all about the money. The investors who handle others' money is all about *their* money. Any business where there are shareholders is *not* all about you. Recently, an airline company gave a well-deserved raise to its employees, and the shareholders made a stink about it.

So, in a nutshell, I advise you to have the same attitude as Del Griffith (John Candy's character in the movie *Planes, Trains, and Automobiles*). He told Steve Martin's character, "Like your work. Love your family." I believe everything besides your family is a freakin' business. You can easily be replaced at work, but not in your family.

Now, going back to these actors and their behaviors I discuss, can you blame them for their actions? I don't mean the ones who commit a crime. I mean the ones who take full advantage of their fame, the ones who are not strong enough or don't know how to stay grounded with their fame. Example: An actor's face was on the front cover of a major magazine with the statement, "Sexiest Man Alive." This actor constantly has his ass kissed by people he doesn't even know. So we, the public, assist in his delusion. How? This actor was inappropriate in a massage session with a female therapist, then the public scratches their head as to why someone would do something like this. It's because we assisted him in his life's distortion.

I have seen the movie *Idiocracy*. When it first came out, I considered it a very funny comedy. I viewed it again under our current administration, and this time it scared the shit out of me. It hit too close to home.

Indeed, there are many people in this industry who are fine human beings. The media, in general, will focus mostly on the negative behavior.

As a society, we also tend to focus on the *bad* behavior of these celebrities. Perhaps it makes us feel better knowing that someone with that much power and money did something that stupid. Then we feel better about ourselves because we know that we would never do something that stupid. However, in chapter five, I mentioned that the judge told the court that the burglar who was in the judge's class in middle school was the nicest kid in the class. So why did the nicest kid in the class turn to crime? Maybe because he was in the position where that was all that he could do.

Why do celebrities lose their moral compass? Because their entire world has become delusional because of how they are treated by the industry and the pressure of what is expected from them.

Years back, some college football players were criticized for selling their championship rings for thousands of dollars. People started to judge the players' morals and integrity. People were quick to judge. They did not know the history of these players/kids who sold their rings and the conditions of their upbringing. These were young college kids, and that money simply meant more to them than the piece of jewelry.

Some of us were lucky enough not to be in a situation where we had to resort to this kind of behavior for survival. We are all hypocrites to some degree. Some much more than others. We all do dumb things. We are not perfect, nor should anyone try to reach for that. You will never enjoy your life if you even strive for perfection.

The best thing I did for myself to enjoy life more was simply to be present wherever I was and let go of all the power I thought I had over others. Life didn't have to be that hard. I became more selective of the rubbish I allowed to enter my mind. Basically, it was an illusion.

Another fact that I learned to accept was that I could not be the best in everything or even the best in my field every day. I realized there will be days when I believe I am brilliant, and there will be days that I believe I am a *schmuck-on-wheels*. That is okay with me. I knew I needed to experience an array of feelings in order to be human.

Armand Goldman

As I mentioned earlier, from my experience many celebrities are not the easiest to work with and are egocentric. But some are extremely pleasant and are a joy to be around. So I'd like to end this chapter on a good note.

I worked at a very small, luxury resort in Scottsdale, Arizona. From the grounds to the casitas, this place was absolutely gorgeous. It was one of my favorite resorts to work at. The spa had a very soothing and calming environment.

When I went to the relaxation area and called my client's name: "Mr. Armand Goldman." A man stood up and walked forward. Because I wasn't certain it was him, I asked him, "Are you Armand Goldman?" In a very calm and soft voice, he said, "Yes." The reason I confirmed his name with him was because I realized he was Robin Williams. It slipped my mind that celebrities often use other names. Armand Goldman was his character name in the movie, *Birdcage*.

We walked up the stairs and into the massage room. Normally, with other guests, in order to have them become comfortable with me, I would ask questions such as, "Where are you from?" But with people who are famous, one doesn't ask that question. However, I always ask the same questions during the intake prior to beginning the massage, like "Do you have any areas of concern?" and "What type of pressure would you like?" These were the only two questions I asked him before the massage began. During the massage I asked him how the pressure was. "Splendid" was his reply.

Heroes—Who Needs Them?

We all know Robin Williams as very energetic, loud, and funny, and that he could never sit still for a second during his TV interviews. But in my massage room, I experienced the opposite of what the public knows him as. He was very soft-spoken with a quiet, gentle nature. Let's not forget, "show biz" is show business, and showing himself to us as we all know him is his job.

Only at the very end of the massage after we left the massage room did he display the Robin Williams we all know. As we made our way down the stairs, he was extremely animated, speaking very fast and loudly. He said a joke, and he started laughing exceedingly. And I also started laughing exceedingly. I just wish I knew what the hell he said! You see, he mumbled that joke out so fast that I couldn't make out what he was saying. I couldn't possibly say something like, "What did you say?" after he already started laughing at his joke. So I just went with it and laughed.

Less than a year later in that same resort, I had a client on my schedule by the name of "Teddy Roosevelt." My spider senses knew it would be Robin Williams again, and it was. That name was his character in the movie, *Night at the Museum*. This time it was a couples' massage with his wife, but with no jokes afterwards.

I can honestly say that most famous people are not respectful of others' time. Even when they show up late, they still want the full massage time they were scheduled for, as though the therapist just came into work that day just to massage *them*.

The fact that Robin Williams, one of the biggest celebrities in the world, showed up on time twice, waited in the relaxation area with other clients respectfully, and was extremely polite to me and the staff says a lot about what kind of a man he was. I wish he was as happy as he appeared to all of us.

11

LUCKY I RAN INTO YOU

Don't count the days; make the days count.

—Muhammad Ali

Years back, a friend informed me that there was a massage therapist position open at a cancer center she worked at. She thought I would be a good fit. I told her, "Thanks, but no thanks." I asked her, "Isn't that a very sad place to work?" She said it was a very rewarding place to work, and yes sad at times. I passed up her offer.

In the past, I had never been comfortable around people who had serious illnesses like cancer. I never knew what to say or even what not to say. Whenever I would be in the presence of someone with cancer, I would feel guilty that I was healthy and they were not. I always thought that if someone was down on their luck, I could give them some money to help them out, however if someone had cancer, I felt I couldn't simply reach into my pocket and hand them some health. Because I felt uncomfortable, I stayed at jobs that I was familiar with—resorts.

Eight years later, I visited the same friend for coffee at the cancer center she worked at. When I arrived, she was standing with some volunteers and a few of the patients. They were all joking and laughing. I didn't know what to make of what I observed. I just stood there alongside them with no expression. When I was alone with my friend, I asked, "Those people have cancer?"

"Yes," she said. "But these patients don't look at life the

same way that your resort guests do." The statement she made was one that I would soon learn for myself was true.

On my first day at work there, my first client was a woman who had stage IV bone cancer, one of the most painful cancers anyone could have. She came in with her friend who was there to help her onto the massage table. I did my intake of questions and let her know I would step outside the room and wait for her to call me back in when she was ready.

While standing outside the door, I heard this woman cry and scream just trying to get on my table. Now I was nervous. I thought, "What the hell can I possibly do that would make this woman feel any better, and could I even lay my hands on her without it hurting her?" I felt as if I was about to perform surgery on a patient when I wasn't even a surgeon. So, I walked into the room just hoping for the best. I started with very light massage strokes, which I kept throughout.

During the massage session, she shared her story. She told me that when she found out she had stage IV bone cancer she was sixty-five years old. Prior to working at this cancer center, I was aware that patients who first found out they have cancer go through emotional stages. The stages are along the lines of *shock, denial, anger, fear, sadness, and finally acceptance.* I believe this woman bypassed most of these emotions.

She told me that when she was first diagnosed, she had a "pity party." Shortly after, she went for a visit to the children's cancer center here in Tucson. After a couple of hours observing these children, she realized how very fortunate she was to get cancer at the age of sixty-five, because these kids wouldn't have experienced as much life as she had been lucky to. She seemed to quickly accept her cancer, and she truly appeared to be okay with it. My friend was right about patients who have cancer. They *are* different from clients at resorts.

Like I said, I was unaccustomed to my new work environment. Most of my clients were already-established patients in treatment, going through radiation and/or chemotherapy, and I was simply the new massage therapist. Most of them had good attitudes and were full of hope. So just being new on this job I hadn't witnessed all the stages that they would go through, at least not yet. Then patients who were new to me started to get scheduled with me. Since I was inexperienced, I didn't say very much, and if I did it wouldn't have mattered anyway because these people who had been just newly-diagnosed were in shock. They wouldn't be present with me no matter what.

Most of these new clients did not speak much during their first couple of massages. They seemed to be still digesting the fact that they had cancer. When they did start talking during their massage, they talked about what they do or did for a living and the positions they held. They didn't typically speak of the present—only of the past.

Once they started treatment, some of them would be much too sick and weak to even come see me. I would often see them in the hallway or in the waiting room waiting to get their treatments. When they started feeling better, they would come back again for massages, only this time the conversations were unlike before. There would be no more talk of the past, no talk of jobs, no talk of positions held, no materialistic talk, and no more talk of status. They would only talk of the present moment. Many of them would start to express their love of nature, like the wildflowers that were starting to grow. Some mentioned getting involved with dog rescues and volunteering. They talked about their cherished friendships and happy memories. Basically, they spoke about the important stuff, with no more bullshit.

For too short of a time, I had a client in her twenties with glioblastoma, a form of brain cancer. This young woman gave off the aura of pure love, extraordinary kindness, with no judgment. Just her eye-contact alone put me in the state of comfort and peace.

She was accompanied by her mom who sat on a chair in the corner of the room reading a book. She needed to be there in case her daughter had seizures. She enjoyed her massages, and I enjoyed her spirit and attitude even more.

She always had a smile on her face, and I would often wonder why and how. Did she not grasp the seriousness of her condition? I thought.

When I first began this career in 1993, I would often hear the word "energy" being thrown around by other therapists—too often, if you ask me. What the hell were they talking about? People have heads, torsos, and extremities, and that was all there was, I thought.

With years of massage behind me, and with going through my own crap in life, I can tell you that *energy* is for real. Massaging her was like recharging my battery. It started the minute I laid my hands on her. It was as if I plugged myself into an energy source.

Not very long after having her as my client, her mom informed me that they would be stopping her treatments. I knew I only had a few more sessions with her. On her last visit with me, she showed up in a wheelchair and still with a smile. I had a strong feeling that this would be the last time I would see her. I remember trying to keep my composure during this particular massage. I positioned myself in a such a way that I was not facing her mom, so she would not witness the tears coming down my face. I could not imagine what she and her family were going through at this time. Needless to say, this indeed was our last session. The first time I massaged this young woman, she let me know that the CD I happened to play was her favorite. I still occasionally play that music, and each time I do I can feel her spirit.

I received a phone call one Sunday morning from someone whose friend was dying of cancer. She was in hospice, and one of her last wishes was to have a massage before she passed. I told her friend that I would not be available until Wednesday that week. "That's too late. She may not be around that long," she said. So I went within the hour.

When I got to her room, there were friends by her bedside saying their last good-byes. Once they left, I entered the room and introduced myself. She was only fifty-two years old. We started small-talk just to get to know each other. I purposefully didn't want to show any pity for her. I just kept a simple smile and kept eye-contact. That may sound cold, however from my experience, many people with cancer at this stage don't really want any pity or any sympathy. What they want is for you to be present and hold space for them.

In the past, I had clients pass away—some old and some young. This was the first time I massaged anyone who only had days to live. Since she could not move, I had to stay on her hospice bed and massage her feet, legs, hands, and arms. We continued talking a bit, and I observed her as someone who was very okay with her upcoming transition. She was soft-spoken and talked about the birds outside her window as she watched them eating from the bird-feeders. She was admiring all the birds and their beautiful colors. She also mentioned the beautiful flowers and trees outside her sliding glass door. This was a woman that was so close to death but yet was so peaceful. She found the pleasure in simple things like nature.

As Albert Einstein said, "There are two ways to look at life. One is to perceive nothing as a miracle, to write everything off as coincidence or blind luck. The other way is to see every burst of life as a miracle, to fall into a state of awe every time you see a budding leaf on a tree or a human taking their last breath."

When the massage was over, we spoke for a short time before I left. I did not say good-bye when I left the room. I simply smiled and said, "Thank you for allowing me to massage you." What else could I say? The following day, her friend who arranged this massage informed me that she had passed away.

Being a massage therapist at swanky resorts is such a contrast from working at cancer centers. It's like living in two different worlds.

Often at cancer centers, I would witness a patient who for many reasons would fall down and be in need for immediate medical attention. When this happens, the staff drops everything and rushes to help in any way they can.

Often at the swanky resorts, I also see the staff rushing

around for a very different reason. An unannounced auditor would visit frequently to evaluate the resort. Once management gets wind of this possible secret auditor, they alert the staff. Management rushes around the resort informing employees to be on their toes. They even go so far as to hand out little pieces of paper with information that all employees need to know in case they encounter this auditor. These little pieces of paper are passed around like a busker's hat at a variety show.

The cancer center staff rushes to save a life, and the swanky hotel staff rushes to gain an extra star or not to lose a star—all in the name of the hotel's ranking.

For the resort guest, their first impression is everything. God forbid I should mispronounce a name. The guest looks at me as if I just insulted his/her mother. What is it with these people?!

First impressions mean diddly-squat for people who have cancer—unless you come up with a cure for cancer.

Five things people regret most on their death bed

I recently stumbled upon an article by the *Business Insider*. The same kind of research is written by many other publications. Somehow, no matter how many people are interviewed or whether they are doctors or ditch-diggers, they all basically give the same answers.

This information is something that should be taught to us in elementary school, reform school, finishing school, and college. It should also be shoved down our throats throughout our lives. I will list them in the same order as the *Business Insider,* and I will add my own thoughts on each:

1. *I wish I had the courage to live a life true to myself and not the life others expected of me.*

As soon as we enter this world, we *are* true to ourselves. We express ourselves and our needs as infants. There is no shame or guilt. There is no need to impress others. We are simply ourselves. As we grow, so too does our consciousness of our behavior. This consciousness stems not from within, but from the external. We now accept this as normal. The by-product of this is depression and anger. Unfortunately, some of us don't realize this until we are older. That is when we begin to reflect and work this shit out—before we check out.

2. *I wish I hadn't worked so hard.*

I wish I hadn't worked so hard too! So what exactly is work? I used *Webster's Dictionary* to define the following words: *work*—a place where you do your job; *job*—the work a person does regularly in order to earn money; *career*—a job or profession that someone does for a long time; *vocation*—a strong desire to spend your life doing a certain kind of work.

So why does *I wish I hadn't worked so hard* always appear on the top of the list of any research in this area? Because not very many of us have a vocation.

I became a massage therapist back in 1993. It started as a vocation for me. I was never as happy at any job until I became a massage therapist. I made good money and massage therapists, in my experience, were treated well by employers. During this hey-day, I gave a massage to a woman who was in the spa industry. She told me, "Your career is going to change drastically. The spa industry is growing at great speed, and massage therapists will be a dime a dozen. You will get paid less, not offered health insurance, and will be treated poorly." At the time, I was thinking I would be retired by the time this happened. I was wrong. This change came like a tsunami.

So, what started for me as a vocation eventually became a career, which then transformed into a job, and now I work. So, I say enjoy what you do. We are all used bullets. From the top salesman who is treated like a king by his employer until he falls into a depression. Or the star running-back who helped take his team to superbowls. Once he has a career-changing injury, he is then obsolete and gets traded. So what does that tell us? Enjoy what you do for a living because you never know...

3. *I wish I had the courage to express myself.*

This almost falls into the same category as number one on the list. We all expressed ourselves as very young children. We didn't need the courage part in this wish. We were trained by our own society to need courage. Why would we need courage to do something that originally comes natural? Much of this topic I covered in my book. I don't want to be redundant.

4. *I wish I had stayed in touch with my friends.*

Some of us do. I feel there is a great difference between people in the corporate world and people who are not. In my experience, people who are not in the corporate world stay close and surround themselves with true friends. They seem happier than the career-minded individuals in corporate life. For those people who chose the corporate life—very competitive, cut-throat, one of extreme stress and sleepless nights—a barrier gets created over time between them and the friends they were once close to. I call this barrier *a career*.

5. *I wish that I let myself be happier.*
The key word here is *let*. So why don't we let ourselves be happier? Are we delaying our happiness until we reach our destinations? When we focus on the journey and not so much on the destination, we find greater happiness.

A hiker doesn't delay his/her enjoyment of the hike until he/she reaches the peak. He/she enjoys the journey from the start.

Some of us wait until shit (bumps in the road) stops happening before we can be happy. Never in my life did I ever witness shit come to a complete halt. There are always tasks and issues to be dealt with in our everyday lives. So, it helps to put that shit on the shelf for now and give yourself a breathing break, and It will be there when you come back, but this time you can handle it with a happier attitude.

A life of comparison with others does not lead to much happiness. We always tend to think the grass is greener in someone else's yard. Keeping up the the Joneses has probably been around since the age of cavemen. I assume they were even comparing their dwellings back then. But this comparison was limited. There were probably only a few in their community. Today, with social media our community consists of over seven billion people. So if we compare ourselves with seven billion people, we will never stand a fighting chance.

Enjoy your personal journey. Focus on your own trail (your own life) without looking around at others'.

So now what? When will the conditions be just right to embark on your dreams, make a change in your life, or begin something that has been on hold for too long?

One day, on one of my long hikes in the middle of the Southwest mountains, I sat on top of a large boulder. I asked myself, "When is the right time to make a change?" I thought about my body and was amazed at how this body of mine can take care of itself and is capable of healing itself without consciously thinking about it. I thought about how my organs function to assist each other in perfect harmony.

Then, I thought about the planet that I live on, how it spins at a crazy speed, and yet I was laying as still as the rock I sat on. This atmosphere has the perfect conditions to sustain life. Our distance from the sun and moon also make it a perfect environment. We have neighboring planets that protect our Earth from getting bombarded by asteroids. I also have technology that not long ago would have been considered infeasible.

So, after thinking about all this, I figured I had that going for me. What more could I ask for? Perhaps time. But I had time, and I didn't use it well.

Then I thought about a Cat Stevens song—*Oh Very Young*. He was absolutely right. We are only dancing on this Earth for a short while.

www.ingramcontent.com/pod-product-compliance
Lightning Source LLC
Chambersburg PA
CBHW032039290426
44110CB00012B/867